Devil's Gold

Ted Falcon-
Barker

Devil's Gold

*"Only two people know
where the treasure lies, myself and the Devil,
and he who lives the longest
can claim it all"*

BLACKBEARD

NAUTICAL PUBLISHING COMPANY

K. ADLARD COLES   COMMANDER ERROLL BRUCE RN (RTD)
Captain's Row · Lymington · Hants

in association with
GEORGE G. HARRAP & COMPANY LTD.
London · Toronto · Wellington · Sydney

First published in Great Britain by
NAUTICAL PUBLISHING COMPANY
Captain's Row, Lymington, Hampshire

Composed in 11 on 13 pt Baskerville
and made and printed in Great Britain by
The Camelot Press Ltd., London and Southampton

Maps and Illustrations

Key to the Treasure Map

1 Deep Water.
2 This mound we thought to be covering part of vessel about 50 feet down.
3 Three cannons over abyss.
4 Wreck of *La Nuestra Senora de la Concepcion*.
5 Reef which shows at Low Water.
6 "Boilers."
7 Yacht *Charon of Styx*.
8 Two cannons with wire lashings used as emergency anchor by *La Nuestra Senora de la Concepcion*.
9 $4\frac{1}{2}$–5 feet at High Water.
10 Large anchor stuck in reef.
11 Sand 10–15 feet. Good anchoring.
12 Safe entry through reef when wind was less than 15 m.p.h.
13 Passage of *Charon of Styx* into reef area.
14 Last path of *La Nuestra Senora de la Concepcion*—approximately 15 feet deep channel.

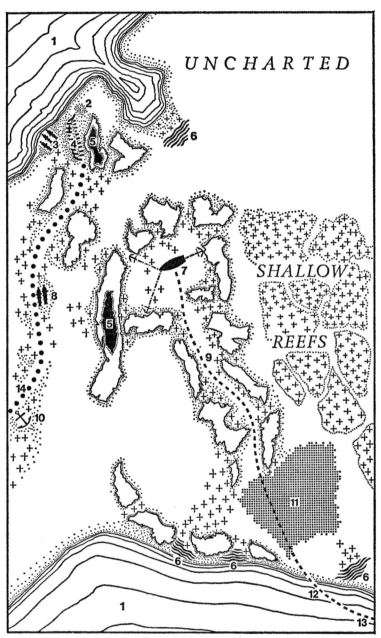

UNCHARTED

SHALLOW

REEFS

Part of Silver Reef

One

The reef was steep, from just below the surface to a ledge sixty feet down, then plunging away into fathomless blue-black depths. The cannons were still there, overgrown with colourful anemones surrounded by tiny tropical fish of every hue, flitting in and out of the razor-sharp coral growths.

I had no compressed air bottles in those days, only a mask and an old lead pipe as a weight belt. With a few friends, I had been sailing round the forbidding coast of Haiti, the dark republic of Voodoo fame. Fishing and sailing was our main aim but our reason for being in that particular area was Barracuda —not that steely-eyed fish, the barracuda—but a young African girl who was known by that name. Some said that she was Voodoo priestess.

I had met her in Port Royal, Jamaica. After some misunderstanding, which had resulted in her trying to stab me with a deadly piece of bone which she always carried about her person, we became friends.

She informed me that she originally came from Haiti and that she belonged to a religious cult whose deity was the barracuda, hence her name. She told some fascinating stories, and we had long conversations over rums and coke.

Later she spoke of her father, a fisherman living on the island of Tortuga, north of Haiti, and how he frequently came home with assorted pieces-of-eight. So when the chance came to go sailing in a well-found, forty-foot yacht, it seemed the natural thing to go to Tortuga, a once infamous pirate haunt.

We had been there four days, and I was swimming, making half-hearted attempts to spear a fish for dinner, when I saw some odd shapes on the bottom.

Sixty feet is a long way down, but after several efforts it suddenly dawned on me that they could only be cannons: cannons could only point to a wreck, and a wreck with cannons in those waters conjured up images of pirates, buccaneers, galleons, and all the fabulous legends of the Spanish Main. From there it was only a short jump to dreams of untold wealth in gold bullion and silver plate.

Unfortunately, the prolific spreading coral had all but covered the vessel; only three cannons and what could have been an anchor were in evidence.

I said nothing to the others, and promised myself that one day I would return.

That was how it all began. Three years went by. It is not often that one gets an opportunity to sail in the Caribbean. But there I was again—this time with four sets of aqualungs.

It had taken quite a bit of persuasion to talk the skipper into altering course on his yacht delivery job to the Virgin Islands. "Just two days, no more," I told him. "All right," he finally agreed. "I've always wanted to dive on an unexplored reef."

I described the wreck, but with the stipulation that it would remain strictly secret, even to him. He was to anchor the yacht and I would go off in the dinghy. If it proved really interesting, then I would return to the U.K. and organize a full-scale expedition in which he would have a share.

"It's Devil's Gold," I told him, thinking of Blackbeard's prophetic remark the day before his death: 'Only two people know where the treasure lies, myself and the Devil, and he who lives the longest can claim it all.'

We shook hands on it, altered course, and solemnly drank the last can of luke-warm beer.

The first day the sea was choppy and I could not find the place. It was well past noon on the second when I saw again the familiar reef. But where were the cannons? Had they been discovered and removed? As I glided closer I suddenly spotted one, and then another, almost completely covered.

Systematically I surveyed the area. The flatter part of the ledge seemed to be covered by a large mound. Was this the wreck? Did the cannons slither out as she settled on her side, sliding to the very edge of the void, over which they still projected, permanently incorporated into the reef itself?

Using an ex-Army entrenching tool—a kind of short-handled combination axe and shovel—I managed to prise pieces off here and there, but most of it felt like granite. It was evident that explosives would have to be used if one was to explore through the various layers.

In a cave-like depression, I saw what looked like an interesting piece of coral and chopped away at it until a piece the size of a football came away in my hand. Then I noticed that other large pieces could be separated.

I made several trips, carrying these over to the anchor chain where I had taken the precaution of laying a large wicker shopping basket. After that it was only a simple matter to heave the whole lot up until the dinghy began to look like a gravel barge.

When my air ran out, I climbed back on board and began to examine the finds. Breaking up the coral, I discovered that these were merely thick encrustations. Inside were unrecognizable remains of what must have been pieces of brass and some circular lead marbles (which I discovered later were musket balls).

Then fell out, for what I fondly hoped would not be the last time, a small tangled mass, a buckle twisted up in a long thin chain. The buckle glinted yellow, and the chain, on being rubbed, was unmistakably gold.

Almost shyly, another piece fell out, a torn and twisted thin yellow band in which a green stone was embedded. It was a two-and-a-half carat emerald, which I later sold for £250.

There was no more air and we had no compressor on board. Calling into Haiti was unthinkable; we knew how highly unpredictable was the reception one could receive in that country.

"There's only one thing," the skipper declared later. "You'll have to go back to England and organize an expedition."

*   *   *

Two weeks before Christmas, 1965, I flew into London Airport, to be met by Jill Reed, a journalist and the best ship's cook in the business. She had received my letter describing the finds, and was excited at the prospect of taking part in another expedition.

Our previous adventure together had terminated in the sinking of my yacht, *Pagan III*, on our way back from the Red Sea, after a collision, and several hours in a leaking dinghy before we were rescued. Jill, by all accounts, should have been like other girls of her age, a steady job, with pay-as-you-go income tax, and a pension at sixty.

But this was not quite her cup of tea; instead she was looking for something different, and a little treasure hunting in the Caribbean was just the ticket. The first step was to obtain a suitable yacht.

Luckily, the Boat Show in London was about to start, which saved me the trouble of travelling all over the British Isles in winter weather looking for a suitable craft. A thirty-foot fibreglass sloop, built by Westfield Engineering of Poole, was exactly what I wanted.

Fitted with bilge keels, she could sail comfortably in four feet of water. With the forecabin, saloon, open cockpit and stern cabin, she ensured maximum privacy for four people, and could take six at a pinch, by sleeping two extra bodies in the saloon. The 15 h.p. diesel, with tankage for up to 1,000 miles, made her reasonably independent of sea and weather.

Delivery was agreed for April 1st, leaving me a couple of months free to plan our future movements.

It was decided that Jill and I would sail the yacht, by then christened *Charon*, to the Mediterranean for trials. An old acquaintance, Hugh MacDonald, was to join us in Tangiers during January the following year; and from there we would cast off for Haiti, an estimated voyage of two months, taking our time.

Meanwhile, at spare moments during the seven years since my discovery of the wreck, I had been researching archives in London and Madrid to discover more about the wreck, and to identity it if possible. After months of examining ancient maps, dusty parchments and log books, I felt I knew the answer.

The wreck I had discovered was, I was almost sure, the ill-fated treasure ship, *La Nuestra Senora de la Concepcion*. It was a remarkable story.

*   *   *

Early in the seventeenth century, ten Spanish vessels formed into an armada for protection from the hordes of pirates and buccaneers then infesting the high seas. Even though loaded down with gold bullion and silver plate, they were heavily armed and no easy prey.

The senior officer was an Army general who overruled the Admiral commanding the fleet. The General wanted most of the treasure loaded on to the largest vessel, where his troops could keep a better eye on it.

The Admiral's view was that, if attacked, some vessels could be taken, and that it was better to risk losing a part of the treasure than possibly risk the capture of the biggest prize.

The General had his way, however, and off they sailed.

Great thought had gone into protecting the vessels, but little into the state of the weather or the conditions of the ships. *La Nuestra Senora de la Concepcion*, commanded by the Admiral, was the most heavily loaded.

Also it was in the worst state.

A hurricane blew up, and the ships were dispersed. Several days later, with his ship dismasted, under jury rig, and in a sinking condition, the Admiral was pacing the deck, cursing the Army. Wallowing somewhere north of Haiti, the only hope was to make land and repair the vessel.

The two pilots on board decided to alter course against the

Admiral's wishes. Traditionally, in matters of navigation the pilots could not be overruled. Disclaiming all responsibility for what might ensue, the Admiral carried out a hand-washing ceremony on the main deck.

The course was altered and that night the vessel struck a reef and slowly sank. Not however, before some of the bullion had been unloaded on the reef itself.

The ill-fated Admiral and some of the crew, taking gold and silver plate, sailed off in a longboat and made a landing on the Island of Tortuga, at a place henceforth named Puerta de la Plata. The Admiral and some others eventually made it back to Spain.

Plans were later made to recover the treasure, but as Tortuga was fast becoming a pirate stronghold, it was not practical.

Years went by until in about 1680 William Phips, the Boston-born skipper of a trading vessel (some said he was trading, others that he was a pirate) heard strange rumours that a neat stack of gold ingots had been found unattended, sitting on a reef.

Deducing that a bullion ship must have gone down nearby, he made further enquiries. So we find him some years later trying to obtain the support of the King of England to mount a full-scale expedition.

His story must have been a good one, for Charles II supplied an eighteen-gun frigate with crew, and off he sailed.

This voyage was unsuccessful. Several mutinies and a year or so passed, before Phips returned to the Court of the new King James II. The frigate was taken off him, leaving him near destitute.

But what happened next? The Duke of Albemarle, together with other gentlemen of the Court, formed a syndicate: whereupon, for a tenth share of the proceeds, the King himself issued a commission making Phips an official treasure seeker, and in 1686 the *James and Mary*, sailed for Haiti, together with a smaller tender.

---

1 *Charon of Styx* in the Pool of London, with Jill Reed in the cockpit, before setting off to search for treasure in the Caribbean.

In 1687 Phips came back up the Thames carrying thirty-two tons of silver and gold bullion besides precious stones.

Such was the amazement at Court (Phips' share was only one-sixteenth, by the way) that the King knighted him Sir William Phips and appointed him the first royal Governor of Massachusetts.

What Phips had recovered was lying in sixty feet of water. The naked native divers only managed to pick up what had spilled out of the hull, even at that time covered with coral growth.

Phips made another attempt on the wreck, but the news had got around, the area was swarming with pirates, and he gave up the effort. As the Maritime Archives of Madrid clearly show, what Phips brought back to England was only a third of the total cargo.

* * *

Before going any deeper into the adventure, it seemed that a closer look was required at the life of Sir William Phips—perhaps thereby unearthing a clue or some item of interest pertaining to his fabulous discovery.

His Nanny says he was kind-hearted and wept whenever he saw a horse maltreated. This could mean that a spark of the Englishman's love for that largely inedible, stupid beast smouldered in his heart; it could also mean that he wept for not being allowed to join in and beat hell out of the thing himself.

I read history with scepticism, and it was with great doubts that I began to read about this poor son of the soil, who by hard work and application gained the friendship of kings, a knighthood, fortune and position—and, as one of his main backers, the Duke of Albemarle.

Looking back, the Duke of Albemarle appeared to have a

---

2 She was a sturdy craft with twin keels, and a skeg for the propeller and rudder; this skeg was damaged on the coral reef when leaving the treasure anchorage.

3 Ted Falcon-Barker with the anti-tank gun which Hugh MacDonald provided for the protection of the boat and her treasure.

B

golden touch. Money seemed to stick to his fingers, and his estates increased threefold and more. In those days no one could stay on the make and live without using a lot of grey matter and jumping on the right bandwagon at the right time.

Was Phips such a simple honest soul, or was he nothing more nor less than a pirate with brains, who was trying to legalize his position to cash in on his ill-gained booty?

Not much is known about him, but some comes from the Reverend Cotton Mather, a personal friend of Phips. From Mather we know that Phips became a shipwright apprentice and finally owned his own shipyard. An Indian raid destroyed the settlement, including the yard, and he sailed to Boston in a small vessel he had built himself.

Stubbornness seems a dominant trait in Phips' character. We hear of him learning to read and write, and paying court to a rich widow who was a few years his senior. This soon led to the altar and, armed with fresh capital, he started anew what was to become one of the principal shipyards in Boston. From this, it was only a short jump to becoming Master of his own vessel.

These were the days when pirates of every kind abounded in the Caribbean. Yet, for five long years, Phips managed to navigate the course, returning to Boston from time to time with cargoes of sugar and rum.

This part of his life seems vague. Some say he traded in timber and salt fish. If he did, then his was one of the few seaworthy, armed vessels of any size so occupied.

It is also possible that Phips led a double life once away from the Puritan atmosphere of Boston and his wife's influence. Perhaps, as well as trading salt fish, he also traded in lead and cannon balls, to the detriment of the sorely tried Spaniards.

In those five years he must have amassed considerable gold and silver, possibly bringing back only small quantities, so as not to arouse suspicion: but what of the bulk of the haul? Phips was an intelligent man. Not for him the short rough-and-ready life, terminating in the hangman's rope or bleeding to death on a sun-drenched deck before being unceremoniously dumped to the sharks, as was then the custom for a defeated foe.

Realizing that he could never use his ill-gotten wealth, he sailed to London with the purpose of obtaining a King's commission, giving him the right to any salvage found, allowing a share for the King, of course.

This warrant could have a two-fold use for a subtle pirate. It allowed him to dig up his own loot and pay a percentage on it, a system well recognized today under the guise of income tax.

It also enabled him to make deals with other pirates, and finally could act as a cover and protection if he were to run across a vessel worth plundering.

And so we see him in a new role, the poor shepherd turned shipyard owner, then salt-fish trader with the tongue and persuasion of a first-class con man. This would mean ample means to dress accordingly, to entertain lavishly, and build up a coterie of followers and hangers-on, until, before twelve months had passed, he finally came to meet His Majesty, the adventure-loving Charles II.

What could appeal more to this august personage than a gamble at finding sunken bullion owned by those onion-eating Spaniards, whom he loathed?

It was common knowledge that, for all the gold and silver taken, much more was lost on the dangerous reef-strewn route, which the unfortunate commanders forcibly sailed to avoid the privateers and freebooters in the safer passages or deep-water channels.

England held uneasy peace with Spain, but it was no breach of faith to go into the salvage business. It was a cheap partnership for the King, whose share was to lend a naval frigate; she was the *Rose of Algiers*—aptly enough an ex-pirate ship captured from the North African Corsairs—fast, seaworthy, and armed with eighteen guns.

Phips signed on his own crew, with a warrant unlimited as to time; this in itself was a singular fact and one which could give rise to suspicions that Phips had perhaps other duties besides that of searching for shipwrecks. In any case, the wording of the commission was never revealed and no record exists as to its contents.

From there on Phips dropped the manners and the garb of a Court gentleman and became what he probably was, a tough seaman of the old school, showing signs more in keeping with a pirate than a representative of the King.

Arriving in Boston to a warm welcome by his wife and friends, the festivities were slightly marred by an attempt on the life of the Treasury official on board, who had been appointed as recorder of the King's share of the treasure. The official fled. Phips pretended no knowledge of the attempt, although it was perpetrated by his own crew. The official prudently did not return to the vessel.

Phips claimed seniority as the King's vessel in the port. Some ships' skippers demurred so Phips opened up on them with his cannons until they agreed. He then billed them for the powder and shot expended.

The picked crew of the *Rose of Algiers* took on the Bostonian police force in an all-out brawl.

Phips joined in and was seen on the side of men knocking down the minions of law and order. Later he used his privileged position of being on the King's business, and the charges were dropped. The town, however, was scandalized.

Finally, to the great relief of the townspeople, he was about to sail when another ingredient was added to the mysterious brew. The vessel *Good Intent* and its Master joined Phips, and they sailed away together.

By some chance, these two vessels arrived on the scene of what undoubtedly must have been an act of piracy. A ship, the *Resolution*, was standing by a new wreck taking off what it could get and there was no sign of the unlucky crew. What did Phips do? First fire a shot across her bows and investigate the dastardly deed?

Not on your life! What he did was to intimidate the *Resolution* which sheered off before superior power, so he and the *Good Intent* (what a glorious name for a pirate!) spent some time recovering 'sums of money' and other goods from the stricken vessel. The haul was not very much, and hardly paid for the time spent. Mutiny, never far below the surface with a cut-throat crew, broke out.

Phips seemed to be well able to take care of himself; the leaders were cut down in the approved fashion.

Later Phips had another mutiny: that time the crew was ashore on a deserted island. Phips threatened them with the big guns and they desisted. He took them to Port Royal—a pirate hang-out if ever there was one. There, Phips picked up another crew and dumped the most difficult of his men. Then he sailed for the Silver Reef to search for *La Nuestra de la Concepcion*.

Was this a blind? Or was he really going to salvage a vessel sunk by himself on a pirate spree earlier in his career?

The fact is, his crew were too difficult. Rather than take the risk of having his throat cut and losing the lot he abandoned the quest and returned to England. But things were different. Instead of a co-operative Charles II, the new King was a no-nonsense character who was bringing back a little system into his lackadaisical inheritance; hangings were not uncommon, and Phips got little change from his new boss.

He was jailed for a short time, but no records seem to exist to show exactly why. He had no ship and presumably little reputation. But the Duke of Albemarle apparently knew something which no one else did. He staked Phips to *two* new vessels and, for a tenth share, the King agreed to make it legal.

A few other influential members of the Court put up some money and, with cargo to pay the way out and a future cargo arranged for the return journey if the whole thing was a failure, the Duke was assured that at least he would not lose on the deal.

Obviously an astute man, the Duke. As for Phips, the fun was over. Either he had to deliver the goods, or go back to salt fish and humble pie in the old home town of Boston, where the people would be only too glad to remind him of his indiscreet behaviour, with the local Police Commissioner probably rubbing his hands and sharpening his truncheon.

But Phips was to have the last laugh of all, when he sailed back up the Thames a year later with his thirty-two tons of treasure.

*   *   *

One thing was certain. The naked divers could not break into the wreck itself, where at least as much again as had been found still lay as an interesting display for curious fish.

This should have been all I wanted to know.

But another puzzling item met my eyes.

In 1694, at St Mary Woolnoth in the City of London, an entry is listed: "February 18 dyed Sir William Phips and was interred in the vault under the organ gallery, February 21."

In 1876 a detailed inventory took place. Phips' tomb apparently no longer existed.

Phips had supposedly died on his visit to England to answer some grave charges against him. He was then forty-four years old and in the best of health. Did he really die? Was some pauper substituted, or did a sum change hands? Did some rich gentleman from the new world settle in some country estate under an assumed name, to live out his days away from the turbulence of his youth?

It was an interesting hypothesis that gave the adventure an extra piquancy.

*   *   *

My research on Sir William Phips and his mysterious life terminated to my satisfaction; there only remained *La Nuestra Senora de la Concepcion.*

Admitted that a pig-headed General had been given charge of the armada, outranking a more experienced and level-headed Admiral, but the vessel sank in only sixty or seventy feet of water. In fact, some of it was still sticking out of the water, resting on a ledge which dried out two feet at low water. The Admiral presumably took a sight or two before casting off in the longboat (leaving a large body of the crew on the reef to the sharks and barracuda).

Puerto de la Plata was a Spanish port only seventy miles away; it should have been child's play to obtain a ship and return to the area with native divers, especially as the wreck carried most of the proceeds from five years of plunder.

Surely it must have been worth salvaging.

A humanitarian might also ask: "What of the men?" Well, life did not count for much in those days, especially with Spaniards. The records admit to over 300 men missing after the shipwreck. The ship carried approximately seventy tons of gold and silver, the latter taking up the most part, besides precious stones such as emeralds, rubies and a quantity of pearls.

The Admiral, it is said, was very ill on arrival at Puerto de la Plata—understandably enough—but one historical account states that on getting back on his feet, his first action was to make a formal request for a vessel and men to recover the lost cargo.

This was refused—very odd indeed—especially as the other treasure ship carrying the remainder of the shipment and the General, Juan de Campos, had sunk with all hands, when nearly home outside Cadiz.

Five years' work and a fantastic fortune had been lost, yet no efforts were made to recover it. It was enough to make one dubious about the whole story. I was willing to be persuaded that a treasure ship did indeed exist on the Silver Reef, or at least there was an ancient pirate ship loaded with booty; but I could not accept the facts as they stood, so I delved further, and came up with what seemed the only possible explanation.

What body of men with unlimited power could take over a going concern and in a few short weeks drive it to bankruptcy? In short, what organization could possibly have a complete monopoly over all the vessels coming from the New World, dictating the times of sailing, the number of ships used, the routes to be followed, the rations of the men, the pay of the crew, all the thousand and one things known as 'ships business'?

Who else, but a Government department.

Could any private enterprise leave five years of its benefits to rot on a god-forsaken reef, unguarded at a time when pirates roamed the seas, preying on even the most meagre prize and even sometimes on their own species?

No, only a body of gentlemen answerable to the State alone could have been so short-sighted. We, living in an enlightened age when Government bodies take over as a matter of course the rigours and dangers of choosing what we are to spend our money on, can readily understand that for forty long years enquiries and counter enquiries took place to discover why the vessel had gone on the rocks. The *casa de contratacion* back in Cadiz required its documentation to follow a well-defined principle.

If Phips' ship was *La Nuestra Senora de la Concepcion*, it was entirely due to the fact that the Admiral had died of boredom over the years, some of the documents relating to the vessel had gone astray, and finally no one knew or cared about the matter.

Well, almost no one.

After Phips' triumphant arrival in London, a piqued Ambassador for Spain handed in a formal protest: "The Spanish monies recovered from the distant reef belong to His Majesty the King of Spain, whose right and pleasure it is to leave his gold where and for how long he likes."

No record exists as to the reply!

*   *   *

After all this research, I came to the conclusion that possibly *La Nuestra Senora de la Concepcion* did indeed exist somewhere on the Silver Reef, but nothing so far proved it to be the one found by Phips.

What was proven to me, however, was that several galleons carrying gold and silver were lost in that area, and that in no solitary case did the Spaniards attempt to recover it.

So there was I, in 1966, the only living being, as far as I was aware, to know the exact location of an ancient wreck from which I had already recovered gold and emerald jewellery of the same period and origin.

Two

"... *down the Thames in a 30 ft. sloop*
on their way to hunt for Spanish treasure
in the Caribbean"

DAILY MIRROR January 14th, 1967

It is a long way from England to the Caribbean, apart from the lonely sea, there is the lack of signposts and old ladies selling pies and hot cups of tea. There are no convenient garages, and if you are in trouble your only way out is hard work or a miracle or two.

Some people shrug and say: "What with the modern materials, anyone can go anywhere, they even row across the Atlantic. The only thing that hasn't been done is to swim it with water-wings, but even that is a matter of time."

What the Press seems to have missed is the fact that every year a surprising number of small yachts leave port and are never heard of again. With this in mind, it was important that we should give the *Charon*, our new vessel, an extensive testing before casting off for the great adventure.

In these days of high speed travel, the idea that anyone might actually enjoy moving through the countryside at speeds varying from four to six m.p.h. would surprise the average person. On being told further that this included all one's personal possessions, several beds, a toilet and a few friends, the person would probably think of luxury caravans but would be bound to exclaim: "Why so slow?"

What most people do not know is that Europe is criss-crossed by a pattern of canals, some disused, but many still carrying commercial traffic from the German Bight to the Black Sea. Most are accessible to yachts.

About the last thing most yachtsmen want to do is to mess

25

about following a channel bordered by trees, with odd houses on the side, being gazed upon by curious inhabitants, barked at, and even outstared by cud-chewing cows in every direction.

On the other hand, if a man can get a few weeks together and wants to sail the blue Mediterranean, he can shorten the distance considerably and gain valuable time by cutting through France, either entering the highly commercial water-way at Le Havre through Paris down to Marseilles, or taking the Canal du Midi from Bordeaux to Sete, near the Spanish border.

It appeared to me that if we cast off from Poole, went to Falmouth, crossed the northern part of the Bay of Biscay to Bordeaux, took the Canal du Midi, cruised down to Barcelona, around the Balearic Islands and returned via the Channel Islands, we should have had enough varied experience to discover any weak spots. At the same time we could have any modifications and alterations carried out by the builders back at Poole.

The launching day arrived, and after Jill and I had poured a few drops of doubtful Spanish champagne on her fibreglass decks, *Charon* was ready to sail away.

We cast off in the early dawn to catch the tide. The B.B.C. weather forecast proved just right, the sun was soon shining bright, and by the next morning we were already ashore in Falmouth buying up stores.

With the right breeze, the average yacht could make Belle Ile in forty hours; from there it is only a hop, step and a swim to Bordeaux itself.

Again the B.B.C. excelled itself; dawn came and, as foretold, thick fog; only a quick D/F radio bearing warned that Ushant lay directly ahead.

Most people give this island a wide berth, with currents up to seven knots and rocks all over the place, but we wanted to see it. So, carefully rounding the point, I entered the bay, avoiding a large patch of rock, and following the chart with great care made my way into the tiny harbour, which dries out

completely at low water; this is no problem when one has
bilge keels which keep the boat upright perfectly comfortably.

Following the rules I hoisted the yellow jack, but I need not
have bothered, there are no Customs on the island, and the
only authority was the Mayor who made us welcome.

A few aperitifs later we returned aboard for an early night.
We intended to make Belle Ile the next day, but when dark
came we were so close to Ile de Groix that we popped in there
instead; another quiet island off the beaten track.

We were getting ready to cast off the next morning when a
fisherman said something about threatening weather; but the
B.B.C. had been adamant that all was very rosy indeed, so I
shrugged and out we went past the rocks into a fresh breeze.

Soon we were pulling in mackerel one after the other, also a
large garfish which few people will eat as the bones turn to a
bright emerald green when cooked. They do not know what
they are missing, as it has a fine white flesh with a sole-like
flavour. Cooked '*au beurre noir*', washed down with a glass of
dry *Vin D'Alsace*, it made a first-class dish, and we were still
picking our teeth when Jill exclaimed: "Look at that cloud, I've
never seen anything like it!"

It certainly looked strange, like a mushroom, purply black,
and was moving rapidly over the water which it seemed to
hide from view. "Just a freak rain cloud—can't be much harm
in it on such a sunny day," I thought.

It came closer, and with it a wind began to howl; there was
just time to reef the mainsail and it was on us like all the furies
at once. Lightning flashed in all directions out of a deluge of
water, while gust after gust laid us almost flat. By the time I had
finished struggling with the sail, our sunny day had turned
into a winter nightmare. We were soaked through, and so was
the boat.

Battened down with oilskins over our wet clothes, I told Jill:
"Never mind, we only have a few miles to go: we can go under
engine and get there before dark."

But I had no sooner started it than a heavy clonk vibrated

through the hull. The engine stalled. Looking around I found that I had run into one of the fish trap buoys which infest the area. Attached below by anything up to 500 feet of nylon line, the buoy can wrap itself round a propeller and bring the most powerful engine to a dead stop.

Having run through a school of large sharks some hours before, I did not feel too much like diving, but that was the only answer.

The water was icy cold, and as the nylon rope had partially melted with the friction, turning into a plastic collar, it took several dives and some time before the shaft was free. This would have been fine, but one blade was badly bent where it had hit what must have been an unusually heavy float. The wind was now a steady six, pushing us back to Ile de Groix.

"Well, that's that, no engine! Can't risk the vibration: we'll have to sail back." We progressed fast, so fast that I had to reef right down. "Can't get past the rocks into the port like this," I told Jill. "Looks as if we'll have to head out and get some sea room for the night."

Jill looked unhappy. She had studied the chart with me that morning and we had both taken note of the treacherous rocky coast; anything north of Ile de Groix is bad enough in daylight, but at night time in a gale with no engine, it's catastrophic.

This it proved to be, and with all sails down I put out a sea anchor to cut down the leeway. With the masthead light on, and the boat closed right down, we tried to warm up under the blankets. It was no use, we were too cold and wet. Every now and again the *Charon* appeared to lay flat on its side while someone slammed it with a sledge-hammer. It was like a colossus in a mad fury picking the boat up and shaking it, until we became dizzy and lightheaded, wondering if this was going to be 'it'.

Clambering on deck to check the sea anchor, I was floored by one wave and was well on my way to sliding out under the handrails, held back only by a snap-hook and rope which I had fortunately made fast just in time to one of the stays. The sea anchor lasted twelve hours and then gave up. What had been reinforced canvas made to hold a thirty-foot lifeboat in a gale, looked a sad, shredded piece of torn sacking.

Nothing more could be done except to go below and hope for the best. Twenty-four hours went slowly by, then the high-pitched scream altered its tone.

"I think it's dropping slightly," said Jill, sitting up suddenly. It seemed so to me. I peered out and saw a buoy blinking about two miles away. We were drifting about two and a half knots, I estimated, and were passing what I hoped was the extreme edge of the Chausseé de Sein.

As the Admiralty Pilot states: "Chausseé de Sein consists of a chain of islands, rocks and shoals extending about twelve miles. . . ."

Forty-eight hours from the time we had so casually sailed away from the Ile de Groix we sailed into Brest and made fast to the wall, dropping off almost instantly into a deep sleep, which could be penetrated only by the consistent hammering of the French Customs at ten the next morning.

With the propeller fixed, and the *Charon* ship-shape once more, we continued on and called into Douarnenez to see the tuna fishing boats. Eventually we made Belle Ile, and after a quick look at Ile D'Yeu—where Marshal Petain was incarcerated and buried—we entered the Gironde River and came into Bordeaux on the tide.

"At last we can get some good, cheap wine," exclaimed Jill as we went shopping in the town. She was wrong; there was no cheap wine in Bordeaux—that is, *French* wine. The cheapest turned out to be Spanish, which must prove something.

For a sailing boat to go through the canals it must first have its mast removed to pass under the hundreds of low bridges. For this one needs a crane, readily available at the Bordeaux yacht club. Once lifted, the mast is lashed to the deck; then as many car tyres as available are attached round the hull in case of collision with a barge or a lock wall, and off one goes.

The Canal du Midi strictly begins at Toulouse, but this is only of academic interest; the actual distance from the mouth of the Gironde to Sete is 363 miles with 118 locks. The first ninety-three miles are river navigation with tidal effects most of the way. Once at Castets one enters the canal system. The locks are antiquated and the canal is not in very good repair. It is only recently, with the increased cost of railways and over-crowded road conditions, that barge transport for bulk freight such as cereals, cement, and gravel has come into its own.

Yachts drawing more than five feet three inches are likely to go aground in the shallow patches.

Following the contour lines, the canal winds its way through some of the most beautiful countryside of France; away from main thoroughfares, only occasionally does it pass through a large town such as Moissac in the fruit country, or a city like Toulouse.

The water is mostly clean, fed from the higher mountain streams. Every village has its waterside washhouse, and farm-wives energetically pound away at their washing literally on their own doorsteps.

The lock-keepers are usually old men or women, and some-times disabled; it is the custom to help with the locking, open-ing and shutting squeaky gates, and winding at the ancient vane handles which often are bent and demand Heraclean efforts. The keepers have the knack and can do it all apparently without effort. Bollards for tying up are sometimes missing, or in a different place. Sudden currents are frequent; to see a wall of rushing white water bearing down as one is only half ready with the ropes is a fearsome spectacle, and many a hardened sailor has been seen to pale at the sight. Most yachtsmen, after one voyage, swear never to do it again!

Jill and I were in no hurry; we stopped to pick mushrooms and fruit by the side of the canal, shot a few wild ducks, and generally made the best of it.

The weather became warmer as we neared the Midi, and by the time Sete was in sight it was already summer. After six weeks of cruising on the Costa Brava and the Balearics, we made our way back to Sete for the return journey.

By then we had got to know *Charon* thoroughly and had tested her for her Atlantic trip and, by this time old hands at the game, we made it to Bordeaux in less than a week. The voyage back to Poole was uneventful, apart from being held up by gales in the Channel Islands.

The builders were waiting at Poole, and the various modifications were carried out. These included putting track on the forepart of the mast to take two sliding boom fittings right up to the crosstrees, where the booms hung down, lashed to the shrouds when not in use. Running before the wind in the Trades, they could be quickly attached to twin genoas, allowing us to move at maximum speed even in light airs, or so we hoped.

The other and more intricate adaptation was the building up of a self-steering unit.

Much has been written about self-steering. The principle is simple: a wind vane is connected either to the existing rudder, or a separate one. If the vessel changes course, the wind turns the vane; in doing so it alters the rudder, which steers the vessel back on to the set course.

Unfortunately, every sailing vessel has its peculiarities; with so many different forms of stern, and every type of rudder from a moon-shaped solid slab of timber to a knife-edged fibre-glass piece jutting down from the trunk with no apparent support. The trouble is that either the vane comes to a grinding halt caused by the friction of unevenly distributed metal parts, or the weight of several tons of water striking the blade is too much for an unstressed section and the whole issue either twists like a mass of overcooked spaghetti or the rudder simply breaks off short.

A sailing friend, Michael Lawes, had been experimenting for a few years on a self-steering unit which he had finally fitted to his yacht *Paola*. It looked robust but fairly ugly in comparison with the stainless steel and bronze units commercially available. But his worked and never broke down, so I found an engineer, Bill Hansford, who had retired from deep-sea trawling to run as a hobby a small workshop at Lymington in the south of England and we went ahead with the help of Michael Lawes. Bit by bit the mild steel pieces, ball-bearings, and angle irons took shape.

Bill Hansford had his own ideas, and by the time his modifications were incorporated the self-steering had improved in looks.

It was with shock that we suddenly realized that winter was well under way; our voyage could be expected to be extremely cold and uncomfortable until the latitudes of the Canary Islands. So we decided to spend Christmas in London, see the latest Boat Show, and leave in January.

Sailing in the English winter is no fun, we discovered, as we ran up the Solent in a force 7 blow, rolled at anchor off Cowes for the night and proceeded reefed right down up Channel with 'Gale Imminent' ringing in our ears from the B.B.C. Another night we spent round Dungeness Point, sheltering from the screaming wind, then across to Calais to pick up a supply of wine.

Christmas Eve found us battling up the Thames Estuary against a westerly gale, making one knot headway with the engine going all out. Finally, at 5.30 a.m. on December 25th, we sailed under Tower Bridge and tied up to Tower Pier by 'Traitors' Gate'. I kicked the slabs of ice off the deck where the spray had settled the night before, and off we went to friends for Christmas lunch.

A few days later we saw the Boat Show and organized our stores. We did not intend to starve: fifty pounds of rice, fifty pounds of beans, besides Bovril, bully-beef, fruit, and soups for cold weather made enough stores to last three people six months.

A letter from Hugh MacDonald—the old sea-dog of indeter-

---

4 *Charon of Styx* in the Gironde River on her way from the Bay of Biscay for sea trials in the Mediterranean.

minate age who was to be our third member on the treasure hunt—insisted on a few cases of Scotch; he volunteered in a very half-hearted manner to come to London if we really needed his help to bring the *Charon* down to Tangiers, where he was spending his time mostly in the sun on the beach.

With the help of the self-steering, I could write back: "Two of us can go round the world if need be; so stay with the sun and wait for us." On Friday, January 13th, as Big Ben sounded the hour of noon, we cast off and headed down river. Photographers and television film units ground away, and somebody kindly opened Tower Bridge as we went under. The sun shone for a brief moment, then the fog started to close in.

"All that publicity: just as well you didn't tell them where it was," Jill said, slipping on her oilskins.

"Well, it's better to co-operate once the story is out: this way they will at least all agree on the place. If I kept quiet they'd all have a guess and we'd be watched like hawks wherever we went."

Jill laughed. "What about when you told that poor man to watch out in the toilet as you had twenty pounds of high explosives under the seat! He thought you were joking!"

That reminded me, and I moved the detonators to the other end of the boat.

Our submarine blasting gelatine was perfectly safe, but detonators are not always stable. If they exploded by themselves they would make quite a bang, but create very little damage; if too close to the explosive, however, they would detonate the lot, and that would be that!

We would need that stuff to remove the coral growth from

---

5 Off the African coast, sometimes as much as ten miles out in the Atlantic, can be seen these strange craft with a box-like container built on top of a long thin keel. The man seen alone in this boat was attacked and killed by a shark next morning.

6 Survival gear laid out in the cockpit to check that all was correct before the Atlantic crossing; it is kept ready for instant loading into the inflatable dinghy in case of emergency.

c

our wreck. We might also need the automatic rifle and shotgun, I thought wryly. Because of the unexpected publicity, there would be problems of security, once loaded with the treasure we hoped to find; however, these could be worked out when the time came, and not in thick fog trying to keep to the middle of the London River.

We had arranged with my cousin, Reggie Harrison, to moor at his wharf at Purfleet for the night. But the tide changed before we got there, and with it came the night. What with the fog on top of it all, we would have missed Purfleet altogether—but Reggie was waiting for us and shouted as we passed by.

We turned and closed in. The current was fierce; it was as much as the engine could handle. As I got closer and saw the water swirling past the large piles, I realized that this berth would never do.

"Go down to the next wharf!" they shouted. I turned the yacht and went on to where a large area of lights lit up several tankers. After a few passes back and forth, a car drew up on the wharf and out stepped the crew from the Purfleet wharf. They guided me in behind some more towering piles. Eventually I managed to get alongside a ladder with the current almost sweeping me under the wharf. Jill frantically tried to push off as a passing tanker threw a bow wave which rolled *Charon* until the spreaders hit the road at the top.

"Sorry! But I'm off!" And casting off a temporary line, I shot her out at about eight knots backwards, passed under another manœuvring tanker's stern, missed a looming heap of piles and went on down river.

"A close one," I breathed thankfully, "but where to go for the night?" A Port of London Authority boat drew alongside.

"Wait for us at the Tilbury Pier and we'll get you a mooring. Have to go up on a job for a few minutes!" called the skipper on his megaphone. Thank God for the P.L.A.—but where was Tilbury Pier? A while later we found it. Going alongside was out of the question with ferries coming and going. I kept the

Charon's nose in the stream and waited for the P.L.A. to come back.

A man called out from the wharf: "Come round the back. You can tie up there!"

More manoeuvring. The back was dark. There seemed to be a small space behind some boats, if only I could turn hard to port with the swirling current against me.

I tried. Suddenly a huge chain appeared in the gloom from the wharf in the middle of the space allocated, disappearing into the turbulent waters. Surely I am going to get stuck on it? But then why are they guiding me here? Various questions flashed through my mind. Sure enough—a grinding crunch and stuck we were.

The tide was going down fast, and with the chain under my rudder there was only one thing for it, however distasteful. Into the river to stand waist deep on the chain; then to push like hell, while the men on the wharf tried to pull *Charon* forward.

After about ten minutes in the icy water, my breath came in gasps, and it looked as if we were there for the night; then a wave from a passing vessel washed over, and with a final heave the *Charon* slid off. At least we appeared to be undamaged, but it was not a very good start. The P.L.A. turned up, and seeing that we were safely tied up, said that they would call in the morning and arrange for a more comfortable mooring. I changed my pants, wondering how I was ever to get warm again and we went to bed, mindful that we had dared to sail on Friday the 13th, that our first day's sailing to the Caribbean had been a chapter of problems, and that we had yet to reach the Thames Estuary!

Three

*"Rivals may beat Australian
to sunken galleon"*

SUNDAY TELEGRAPH February 12th, 1967

It was morning by the clock but very dark outside when the Port of London Authority officer called. It seemed that there was a tidal basin owned by British Rail at Gravesend which had long been used as the site of the local yacht club. I went over on the ferry and called on it.

A friendly lot were the members, only too happy to let us use all the club facilities and leave our yacht as long as we liked. The only charge would be to British Railways whose property the basin was and who supplied a lock-keeper to open the gates.

As soon as the tide was high enough, we got out from our perilous moorings, and giving the chain a wide berth, set off across to Gravesend. The fog had come down again, but I had taken notice of the position of the buoys when visiting the club in the morning and entered without difficulties. We spent all day packing our various stores ready for sea; the original plan of having all the tinned goods in the stern cabin had to be abandoned as the vessel lay too deeply in the water aft, while the bows rose correspondingly too far forward. Then we went for a final night out on the town, picking up the mail on the way.

In it was an urgent letter from Hugh MacDonald. A real smack in the teeth. It was a long story.

A French fisherman friend of Hugh's had met a bunch of roughnecks who in a drunken moment had confided that they owned a diving boat which they were taking over to Haiti on a treasure hunting expedition.

36

This in itself was an interesting coincidence until later they further mentioned that an English group with a small sailing boat was also going to the same area. They knew that this boat would be calling at Lymington, and one of them was in contact with a friend there who was to advise on the date of sailing.

Their vessel was powerful and might be capable of nine knots crusing speed. They intended to sail to the Canaries and there wait for the unsuspecting yacht.

The plan was first to let the yacht sail with a good start, then follow it to the area north of Tortuga Island, for which they seemed certain we were heading. I had made no secret of the area, feeling that finding an almost invisible wreck in reef-infested waters miles from any landmarks would be beyond most people.

Hugh MacDonald, with his connections, had soon found out about the group. A first-class bunch of cut-throats led by a man who had been in the smuggling racket, graduating to arms and drugs. Even this had become too hot for them, and with time on their hands and a well-found vessel, they had hit on this new plan.

The idea that some other searching vessel might poke around my area did not really disturb me. But a shipload of armed gangsters was something else. They could double our speed for one thing.

Hugh suggested skipping Lymington altogether. Instead, going straight down to Tangiers to pick him up, then cutting across to Madeira, giving the Canaries a miss. He also mentioned that he could get his hands on a three-inch mortar or a Boyds anti-tank rifle, cheap.

I said to Jill: "The problem is, as soon as we disappear the bastards will work out how long it will take us, realize what we are doing, and act accordingly. If they have a contact in Lymington, he'll probably talk to the yacht people and ask them when we are due. We had better write and say that we are held up for a start."

It was evident that we could give the winter weather as an

excuse for waiting until later in the year; but it would still take us two months to get there, and with a deep-sea vessel like theirs it would be child's play to find us.

I could only see two probabilities. (*a*) Go over wherever they were, and stick a charge in the bilges when they were out carousing; (*b*) make as fast a passage as possible direct to Haiti and hope for the best.

The first appealed to me the most, but seemed a little drastic. Then I remembered an old sage I had met in Ceylon years before. He said: "Why struggle with your problems—forget for a few days. He who lives inside you will work it out; suddenly one morning the solution will lie there in your mind."

Leaving the *Charon* snug in the basin, we moved into my cousin Reggie's bungalow for a few days of meditation, good food and wine.

Lying in the bath a few days later, my toes under the hot tap, with Jill furiously hammering at the door, I remembered something Reggie had said. We had been talking about how cold the first few weeks of the voyage would be, and he had said: "Why don't you just get the *Charon* heaved on to the deck of a cargo boat going to somewhere warm, then you'll be half-way there without any effort." I had laughed at the idea at the time.

"You'll be half-way there!"

That was it! And I leapt out of the bath, drowning all the morning newspapers.

"I'll let you know within the week," said Reggie, who was in the shipping business. Later he telephoned from his office: "Is Dakar all right?"

A few days later, there was another call. A seaman friend of Hugh MacDonald had arrived with a parcel for me. "What's in it?" I asked.

"Can't tell you over the phone, mate. But it's a crate about six foot long and weighs nearly a hundred pounds."

Sounds like a coffin, I thought.

"My ship's leaving on the tide, but I'm leaving it on the wharf with X. All you have to do is go alongside and pick it up —the sooner the better."

Obviously by leaving it on the wharf the Customs would take no interest in it, and as long as it was picked up and taken straight on to the *Charon*, no one would care, especially as we were due to go 'foreign' any minute.

"What do you think Hugh's sent us?" I asked Jill. She uncharitably thought that it might be booze, but it looked illogical to send booze to England all the way from Tangiers, especially as bonded stores would be obviously cheaper in England. We picked it up, and feeling rested after a lazy week, we bade goodbye to Reggie and Jean, his wife, then sailed out of our little heaven at Gravesend, heading up the Estuary towards Burnham. From there we intended to keep in touch with Reggie by telephone for news of a ship to Dakar, and meanwhile explore the marshes, perhaps shoot a few ducks or some of the huge hares said to abound in the area.

We anchored for the night in one of the offshoots of the River Crouch, and I opened the crate which was very heavy and well bound with steel straps. I levered away the top boards and saw that when Hugh MacDonald said something he meant it. Resting well-protected by greased paper lay an anti-tank rifle together with fifty rounds of ·55 ammunition; it was not the latest thing for tank warfare, perhaps, but lethal enough at a mile or so, and certainly more than enough to keep off any inquisitive vessel less armoured than a warship.

"He's gone mad! What do you think the authorities would say if they came across that lot?"

"Well, they didn't, and I'm sure Hugh meant well," said Jill.

A gale was blowing. There wasn't much point in moving on that day, and as the area was completely deserted, I decided to try out my new weapon. An old oil drum at 300 yards on the furtherst bank seemed to have been placed there by providence. I lay down on the foredeck, and loading the clumsy weapon with its oversize cartridge, took careful aim. There is nothing like bitter experience to teach the unwary. With a sound like the crack of doom, it kicked me back about three feet: several inches of skin disappeared off my elbows as if by magic as the non-slip fibreglass surface rasped along my arms.

"Never mind," said Jill, with apparent solicitude, "at least you did hit the drum."

I oiled the monstrous thing and lashed it down on the forward bunk for further experimentation when my elbows would be functioning once more.

It was still blowing, so we decided to sleep in next morning. It was barely daylight when a vessel was heard approaching with loud toots. Then several loud thumps resounded on the deck above my head. As we stuck our heads out of the hatch we saw a fishing boat passing by with the laughing crew throwing freshly caught herrings into the cockpit. It seemed too much to go back to bed, and I was cleaning my teeth when Jill spotted another boat coming alongside. I swiftly slipped on a pullover and poked my head out. This time, it was a Coast-guard. He told us that most of the area was restricted and came under the control of the Atomic Energy Commission.

"That's all we need!" I thought. "Here we are with an anti-tank rifle and explosives . . ."

Telling him that we were going to Burnham for supplies, I left it at that. Later he was waiting at Burnham, and very co-operatively guided us to a mooring. I tried to obtain a chart ashore but failed, although it was a well-known yachting centre.

To make up for that, a good engineer—a vanishing race—and I spent the rest of the day cutting three feet off the alloy booms which had proved unmanageable in heavy weather.

*   *   *

I phoned Reggie, who had a friend with a ship bound for Dakar, sailing in the next few weeks; but so far the cost of loading and unloading, especially in Dakar, was not known. It looked a good possibility, so meanwhile we decided to lose ourselves for a bit in the marshes on the other side of the restricted area.

Interesting they were—those marshes. Hundreds of wild black and white geese, and even more species of duck. All were very wary, unfortunately. Having the shotgun at the ready, we tried to get close enough, but with loud honks of derision they always flew off just in time. Every now and again an earth-shaking bang would come from the restricted area, where no doubt somebody was trying out yet another means of wiping off the human race. It seemed a pity in this wild spot that on every hand signs would suddenly appear: 'Beware Danger Defence Dept.', 'Keep Out', 'Danger Dogs Keep Out'. Red flags flying on some of the bends made one wonder what was likely to zoom by. Nothing did—perhaps luckily for us.

January 25th was Robbie Burns Day. "One thing for sure," said Jill, "Hugh MacDonald will be well and truly on the whisky tonight, and doubtless stuffing himself with haggis as well."

"Well, what's wrong with haggis? As a matter of fact I have arranged for half a dozen to be sent to us before leaving. We can drag it out on Hugh's birthday."

"Haggis won't keep in the heat, surely."

"Nonsense, it's full of herbs and things—like salami, it'll keep."

That night we took the ground between an island with a 'Keep Off' sign and another with a sign about oyster fishery, which sounded a little more civilized.

The weather for the next few days was almost spring-like. The sun came out, geese still appeared in great numbers, but kept well away. Even the ·22 with its telescopic sights was not equal to it. A goose at 150 yards is not much of a target from a moving boat. Ducks also flew about again tantalizingly out of range. Apart from that, we had a few days observing the various birds and exploring the scattered creeks and waterways.

More loud explosions in the distance warned that the 'Keep Out' signs were not there for nothing.

The month was almost over when we returned to Burnham.

This time Reggie had some definite news. It would cost fifty pounds for the crane in Dakar, and about ten more for loading dues in the Tees.

At this price the enterprise appeared more than probable. We made a date to meet in London for a final decision, and on the strength of it sailed further north to Harwich. The trip to the Tees up the east coast in February could have its problems, so it seemed sensible to use the good weather while it lasted.

A few hours out and the fog came down cloying our lungs, and about as impenetrable as a pub door after closing time. I decided to anchor in shallow water where large vessels would be unable to find us, but turning almost rammed one of the pirate radio ships, three of which had at the time made their home close to each other three miles off the Essex coast.

I made for the stern and moored, while Jill brewed the tea. The wind came up, dispersing the haze, and a few hours later we continued on our way. Harwich seemed a very commercial port and not the sort of place where I could safely leave the *Charon* while I went to London.

As we were trying to find a suitable anchorage, our echo-sounder battery gave up just at the crucial moment. We drove into soft mud, and finding it impossible to back out, decided to stay the night.

We dried out standing upright on the two keels and, if anything, were more comfortable than at anchor. Before dawn, at high water, we sailed, with a fair wind; this dropped as usual just as Lowestoft, with its narrow tricky inlet, came into view. The waiting fog descended almost immediately, so we entered like an apparition, missing the lighthouse by a hair's breadth. The local yacht club's moorings were very safe, and I made a quick return trip to London.

*   *   *

The die was now cast. To Dakar from the Tees—if we could get there in time. The weather, already unusually warm for the time of the year, had begun to break up. While waiting for the wind to come down to reasonable limits, I managed to get the local riggers to make up two slings with a twelve-ton breaking load; the *Charon* only weighed five, but one must have a measure of safety in these things. A boat-builder made two spreaders out of three inch by ten inch timber, so that the sides of the yacht would not be crushed when the crane started to lift her.

With the enormous coil of galvanized wire in the cockpit, and the two twelve-foot long timbers lashed to each side, the *Charon* began to look intriguing; at the same time, the extra load and its precariousness made it even more imperative to pick the weather.

Off we went again, this time to Blakeney, near the entrance to the Wash. The channel leading into this place is not to be recommended for the faint-hearted. About five feet deep at low water, it winds its way several miles through acres of marshland and sandbanks. Once inside, a large pool, which could accommodate a hundred yachts, lies sheltered from any weather. Seals play where the channel joins the sea, and the waves break on bar; one approaches this at an angle, swinging between two sandbanks, with a few inches below the keel. Calm weather and high water are recommended. We made it at low water with a south-east gale on the make. Very interesting. A wild desolate place, where people are seen only when the tide runs out, coming to gather mussels.

Taking the shotgun we went for a walk. Hares ran out from under our feet, and even partridges flew up as we strolled. Not too approachable were thousands of wild geese, ducks, and other water birds—some of which we had never seen before. I shot a young hare, which was slowly simmered on the kerosene heater in a litre of wine, with tomatoes, carrots, onions, and lots of garlic. It kept us going for the next two days. Leaving Blakeney was difficult; first because we liked the place, secondly the sea was not helpful and we were glad to find ourselves in deep water without once hitting the bottom.

A south-east gale blew up as we made it to the Humber

before dark in record time, and anchored just inside the light-house, rolling heavily until dawn.

The North Sea was living up to its winter reputation. A general forecast of gales throughout *all* sea areas warned us that this was not the time to continue. Regretfully we made for Grimsby a few miles up the Humber.

We tied up to a Belgian fishing boat whose crew were busy pumping out ten tons of water shipped in the forward hold during heavy seas, then we went ashore for some shopping. On our return, seeing that the boat was being picked up and literally dashed into the trawler by large rollers, we immediately cast off, barely having time to thank the crew for a large bucket of whiting and Dover soles.

The next two hours were hell as we precariously manœuvred around trying to find a way to get into one of the locks. The fishing harbour just would not have us. "No yachts," they said helpfully.

Rolling heavily with a two-to-three-knot current sweeping us on to perilous-looking piles, a screaming wind, heavy swell, and falling darkness, we were having a thoroughly alarming time.

Having another try at the main lock, we found ourselves being set against a wall on one side and a large dredger on the other, with no room to turn. The bows couldn't push against the gusts. We looked likely to be flattened against the gates like a gnat on a car radiator but at that crucial moment the lock-keeper, as if by magic, opened the gates.

We flew in at such speed that only full astern saved us from ploughing into the gates on the other side. The harbour inside was calm and peaceful, and there we stayed two days, until the 6.45 a.m. B.B.C. weather report came out with 'Humber south-east force 7/8 veering south 4/5'.

The entrance to the Humber wasn't exactly pleasant, but with the possibility that the wind would turn to help us there was no call for apprehension. That was, until a break in normal radio transmission warned of a blow 'up to severe gale, force 9'. Too late, alas! We were already well up the coast with the tide behind us. Bridlington, a little further up, looked like being possible by nightfall. Clocking over seven knots, we arrived abeam about 4 p.m. but by then the sea was so high that we began to surf in as we approached the unprotected shallow entrance.

Nothing for it but to work out to sea again and have a bash at making it round Flamborough Head. There the sea was confused and unpleasant. A huge cross swell threw us around, and the steering became extremely difficult.

The B.B.C. chose that moment to give out more gale warnings —this time in the Tyne area, which begins just round the Head. 'Up to storm, force 10', they said. Jill did not hear it, so I kept quiet. From the galley cupboards came ominous sounds of breaking glass, and a messy looking juice—eggs and jam by the look of it—was oozing out on to the saloon mat.

What worried me was the thought of the two large timber spreaders lashed each side of the deck; they were all right as long as the ropes held, but once loose it wouldn't bear thinking about! The fibreglass hull was enormously strong, but a battering from one of those timbers would be some punishment. Night fell as we rounded the lighthouse.

Our only safe harbour was now Whitby—another twenty miles up the coast. Rather than enter it in the dark, I decided to press on right to the Tees. There seemed no choice—or so we thought. Suddenly a searchlight was trained on us. I thought it was some sort of patrol boat and downed the main, keeping steerage way with the storm sail. We still seemed to be flying, and it looked as if whoever it was would have trouble catching us up. On the other hand, I was not very keen to go forward on the slippery tilting deck and do battle with the sail. It slowly drew alongside, about forty feet out, and I saw that it was a lifeboat, complete with crew in life-jackets.

"Are you all right?" they called over a loud-hailer.

"Sure! Thanks!" I shouted back into the wind.

"Where are you making?"

"Up the coast."

"You'll be all right in Scarborough. We will escort you!"

"No thanks! We are all right!"

But they did not appear to hear. After about ten minutes of shouting, my voice went and I gave up. "Looks as if we are stuck with them; let's go on," I told Jill. A few miles further on and the navigation lights were still close behind us. Meanwhile, I was thinking—"It's very nice of them, but we don't want to go to Scarborough. Anyway, I don't see how I would safely get in with this sea, and not knowing the port. It will probably be like Bridlington only in the dark. Better go to Whitby as planned."

I heaved to, and again tried to get my message over. "You'll be all right in Scarborough," was all the answer I could get, and gave up.

Scarborough lights appeared, first as a distant glow in the sky then individual lights. There was no electricity cut that night. As we approached, the lifeboat pulled closer and the loud-hailer shouted "Good-night!" I thanked them, thinking what a great body of men they were who would cheerfully take a boat out in gale weather and then escort someone a couple of hours or so just to see that they did not get into any trouble—even if we were escorted to where we had no wish to go!

This was slightly different behaviour from other European countries where lifeboat institutions are mainly non-existent. It reminded me of the time in the South of France when a plane crashed into the sea. The local lifeboat was called, but the coxswain could not be found. He was the one with the ignition key to the engine. After a thorough search throughout the bars of the town, he was found and hurriedly driven to the harbour. Horror! He had forgotten the key! Another panic—it turned up in a drawer at his home: a race back to the boat. Switch on, press the button—silence!

The batteries were flat. New ones were obtained. Precisely four hours after the call, the lifeboat sailed out on its errand of mercy. The plane had sunk by then, not surprisingly, and all the crew were lost.

Moral: keep a life-raft handy cruising in foreign waters.

"Now for Whitby," I said, watching the lifeboat stern light disappearing in the waves. Suddenly an unearthly metallic voice boomed out of the darkness.

"Ahoy there! Have you been into Scarborough before?" And another lifeboat was pulling in alongside. Jill laughed helplessly.

"No, I have not," I yelled above the wind.

"Then follow us."

Scarborough is a fine town, and winter is probably the best time to see it. All the Scarborough Rock stalls, ghost trains, bingo halls, cafés, and garish waterfront amusement stands are closed, their whitewashed windows gazing blindly at the fishermen and their gaily-coloured boats crowding the side of the harbour as if they own the place. Which they should. The lighthouse-keeper was serene and warm in his room at the bottom of the tower on the quay. The yachts in the other part of the harbour lay sadly finished and laid up for the season, while on the hill the dark walls of ancient battlements brood over the scene. I liked Scarborough, and so did Jill.

*   *   *

The Press descended upon us before we could really get down to having a good look at the place. In broad terms the question was; "Why did we turn left out of the Thames, instead of right towards the Bay of Biscay?"

I cursed whoever was responsible for calling out the lifeboat. Now there was no hope of keeping our movements secret.

We sailed for the Tees direct, hoping to pass unnoticed in that commercial maze of wharves, ships and the miles of teeming river traffic. But the Press was alerted, and were waiting to pounce. Pulling into a pier after an uncomfortable night at anchor near the Mouth, I stepped ashore to get the Sunday papers. A man stepped forward with a camera, another with a notebook. We cast off and moored further up river. Two more arrived. So much for our hopes of secret departure!

The *Thackeray*, which was to carry us to Dakar, was due in a few days and would sail almost immediately. This meant that with normal luck we would be diving on the site three weeks later.

One great advantage was that we would be arriving with our six months' supply of food and water virtually intact, and should be able to remain 'working' for at least two months without having to worry about the competition. According to Hugh's latest letter, the gangster and his mates were giving their main engine a top overhaul. Even if they heard about our latest move, it would still take them that amount of time to get over there.

I had asked Hugh to come to the Tees to join us there—but no. The Tees, he said, "was close to Scotland but too far south of the border for a true Scot". He followed on with something about coming elections—a subject close to his heart; the Nationalist Party, he said, were being hamstrung by the bloody English as usual, so he would join us in Dakar and that was that.

*   *   *

Our mail finally caught us up, and in Jill's letter from her mother was a newspaper cutting. I stared in disbelief. It was a full-page feature in the Daily Mirror: 'Man with a Fifty Million Pound Secret'.

Alexandre Korganoff, with two vessels and twenty-eight persons, was to sail to Haiti in April. Aim: to work on *La Nuestra Senora de la Concepcion*. There followed descriptions of the sinking and the treasure on board.

Korganoff I had met in Paris years before. He had contacted me to see if I would be interested in putting up some money

---

7 A quiet night in the Cape Verde Islands.

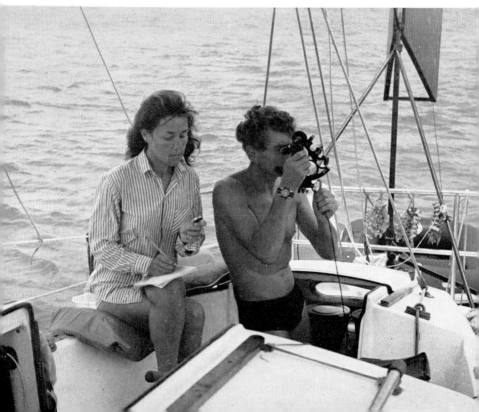

and time to work on the vessel. I was curious, as his description of the fabulous treasure ship and how he had discovered it some years before, tallied with my story. Even the topographical details were similar. But in his case the crew had mutinied, and the expedition had terminated in disaster. Even after losing the vessel and crew, he had carried on with another boat—but still nothing came of it. A further attempt, using metal detecting devices, failed as the instruments did not come up to expectations.

He had been dogged by incredibly bad luck, and was trying hard to get another expedition together.

After hearing his account, I had suddenly realized that *my* wreck might actually be the one he was looking for. But I kept quiet, probably just as well, although Korganoff appeared a gentle bookish fellow and I rather suspected he was more interested in the historical aspects than a serious treasure hunt.

We had discussed the various means of recovering the cargo from under the coral growth of 400 years. But Korganoff appeared unrealistic to me, his ideas requiring an over-large capital outlay—something like £50,000 of ships and equipment—and, what was worse, involving countless numbers of people.

My idea was to use a small vessel and as few persons as possible, employing explosives. My last letter not having been answered, I went my own way.

But there he was popping up again, going ahead with the old method, attempting to recover treasure with treasure. I was doing it the cheap way. Time would tell who was to be right, and this was another reason for getting there fast. I wondered if he knew about me, also if the gangster knew about him. The future looked interesting.

---

8 Jill experimenting with a solar still in case of serious water shortage later. Salt water is poured in at the top and, as condensation takes place inside, fresh water is sucked from the bottom.

9 Navigating by the sun, with Jill taking the exact time as Ted observes the precise altitude with the sextant. Note the drying lobster tails hanging on the rail—caught in the Verde Islands.

D

Four

"Treasure hunt yacht waits for lift"

DAILY EXPRESS February 20th, 1967

The *Thackeray* was bound for Dakar with a cargo of phosphate. She was a far larger vessel than we had expected, and she lay at Billingham Wharf in a dust cloud of phosphate all day and all night. The tall crane dropped its huge bucket in the holds and up again on to the conveyor belt, then down again. The wind, which was bellowing down the river, lifted up the gritty sand-coloured stuff and threw it from one end of the ship to the other.

We came alongside and tied up, and in no time found ourselves in a dust-storm. Phosphate had an ominous sound, and after getting several eyefulls I began to wonder if we were about to be blinded for life. I need not have worried. This phosphate was merely quarried from what had once been the bottom of the ocean, mainly the remains of countless sea creatures from prehistoric times. By some mysterious process, I.C.I. converted this into fertilizers—quite harmless, except on machinery, on which it worked just like sand.

Captain John Wood, a merry Scot, told us to make ourselves at home and gave us the Electrician's cabin with apologies, as it was the only vacant spot. This was four times larger than *Charon*'s saloon, equipped with beds, central heating, reading lamps, a writing desk, settee, hanging cupboards, drawers everywhere, and a hand-basin with hot and cold water. It was to be our greatest luxury for a long time.

The *Charon*'s mast was unstepped using a gangway derrick, while the I.C.I. mobile crane heaved us on to the deck, where

50

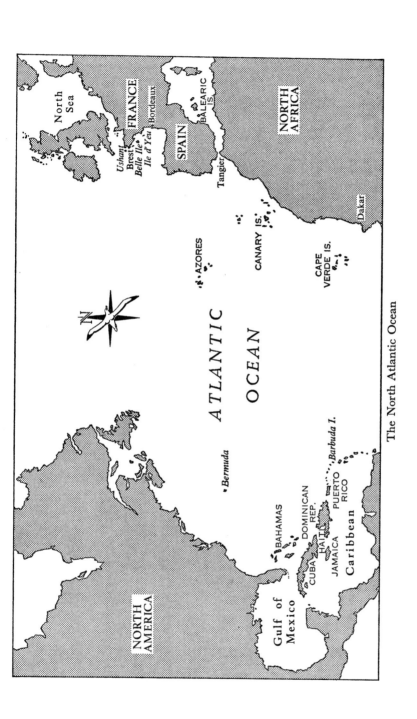

The North Atlantic Ocean

we fitted with only four inches to spare, after great holding of breath as she was lowered past a very nasty jutting piece of metal and the slightest lurch would have punched this straight through the hull. No sooner was that done when an out-of-breath television camera-man arrived. "Sorry I missed the loading," he said, "would you mind doing it again?" He blushed at the reply, but being a true professional carried on shooting.

I had wedges and lengths of three-by-four ready. As the ship sailed down the river with the tide, I hammered these into place and lashed *Charon* down ready for the gales, forecast with great regularity by the B.B.C.

But I should have known better. This time the sea was as flat as a millpond all the way. Every day the sun shone stronger; Jill washed down the *Charon* inside and out, while I got it ready for the anti-fouling. With the help of the Chief Engineer, Ray Jones, I made improvements to the self-steering by adding more grease points, shortened the booms to 14·5 feet which seemed a workable length for running before with the twin genoas, and generally brought the *Charon* up to first-class condition.

The *Thackeray* was a happy ship; cups of tea at 7 a.m., breakfast at eight, morning coffee at eleven, lunch at noon, afternoon tea at three-thirty, high tea at five, sandwiches and tea at nine. I have never had so much regular food at such odd hours, or so much tea in my life. Everyone went out of their way to help us.

It came to me that perhaps we had hit on the ideal way of ocean voyaging.

*   *   *

At 11 a.m. on Saturday, March 11th, the *Thackeray* passed the hundreds of native fishing canoes precariously bobbing up and down off the entrance of Dakar harbour; she moved straight into her familiar berth under the phosphate loading chute. The hatches had already been opened and the last mooring line was still being tightened up when the phosphate began to pour into the holds. Not one minute lost. The skipper reckoned on being back at sea within eight hours if all went well. Meanwhile, the agents arrived with the news that the only crane available was a floating one, which could lift sixty tons, fifty-five more than required.

This monstrous object soon appeared, and it was time for me to arrange the slings. The air was thick with billowing clouds of phosphate; the natives on the crane gesticulating and trying to make themselves heard now and again, disappeared in clouds of dust. It was down my throat, in my hair, and the *Charon* was inches thick with it.

Unfortunately, the crane had a huge hook, too big for our slings; the natives shrugged and all sat down. If it had not been for John Wood, the skipper, we probably would have never been unloaded, but he found some shackles and made up a strop adequate for our weight.

An hour later *Charon* was at last in the water alongside. Then began the business of stepping the mast. Eventually that was up, but when my back was turned one of the boys off the crane decided to shin up it—the stays had not been made fast, and it was a close call. Safe alongside the wall, we breathed a sigh of relief and returned to the *Thackeray*, just in time before she sailed, to try and wash the phosphate out of our hair. It took all the next day to remove another two or three hundredweights of the stuff from the yacht.

Now, what of Hugh MacDonald? The agents knew nothing about him and obviously he had not arrived. Presumably he would be on his way. Meanwhile, we gave the local markets a visit. The prices were high for almost all foodstuffs, but locally grown fruit and vegetables were slightly cheaper than in the U.K. With our six months' supply of canned goods, they were all we required. We stacked the stern cabin with bananas and pineapples, and took on twenty pounds of green tomatoes— enough to see us through six weeks or so.

Three days passed and we were ready for sea, and had even given the self-steering a good try out. It worked perfectly, and while trying it we caught on our line a four-pound fish, which we couldn't identify. None of my reference books showed it— the nearest placed it as one of the tuna family. However, baked with egg plant, tomatoes, and sprinkled with lime juice, it wasn't too bad—but not up to fresh tuna quality. The winds were steady force four or five from north, and it looked as if we should make a fast crossing with no problems.

The Cape Verde Islands, 350 miles away, were scattered across our route and would make an interesting diversion, but if Hugh didn't hurry up we would have to forget about this. The fourth day, the agent had a letter for us. Hugh, at last! He had signed on a cargo vessel calling at Dakar, and it had been held up for a couple of days. "Have you heard that the Nationalists have had a big victory recently? The day's coming when we'll be out from under the heels of the English . . ." Obviously Hugh had not changed.

"Wait till he sees those bottles of whisky, and what a shock he'll get when I serve him up that haggis!"

I had my doubts. It was all very well for Jill to think that she could serve up a haggis at sea, especially as the tropical weather was likely to have detrimental effects before Hugh's birthday came up on April 10th. The last time that I had glanced at the haggis, it had been covered with a kind of furry growth, mixed with phosphate dust. I conveniently omitted to mention that it had been my idea in the first place!

Anyway, the whisky was sure to be appreciated. We had two dozen, and some gin for ourselves.

We sailed out and anchored just outside the harbour in a corner in front of a swimming club, wide open to the weather from the south, but as there seemed to be no weather from that direction at that time of the year, we were quite safe. We spent the next few days fishing with moderate success, but the area did not live up to what we had been told by the locals: "Lots of barracuda, sharks in great numbers, you just throw a line out and in comes a fish." It took us a good four hours of trolling to catch one fish. As for sharks, we never saw one.

On Saturday, March 18th, exactly one week after our arrival, we sailed back into Dakar harbour. Hugh was about due and so was the *Tennyson*, another ship belonging to the same shipping line as the *Thackeray*, and she might have some mail for us. No sooner had we tied up than Hugh appeared to take our lines. "Thought you might have gone without me," was all he said; then, "She looks bonny enough." It was his first sight of *Charon*.

"Well, there's your cabin aft . . . that is after we move some of the bananas," Jill told him.

"I'll move in tonight, have to pick up my gear. When are we sailing? I'll have to jump ship—so the sooner the better."

"Tonight as soon as we see if the *Tennyson* has any mail for us."

"See you then." And off he went.

"What does this 'jumping ship' mean?" asked Jill.

"It means that he has signed for a voyage—perhaps when drunk. I'm not sure if the skipper would let him sign off here; but in any case, he'd better keep out of sight. I think that in these cases the police have the right to pick him up and return him to his ship."

"Won't that spell trouble?"

"I don't know. Hugh only signs on when he feels like it. He usually works on yachts where it doesn't matter. Anyway, if we pull it off, he'll not have to work again."

The *Tennyson* had some mail as we expected. We took a shower on board, the last for a long time probably, and as dawn broke and the hawk-like vultures began to swoop about for their first meal of the day, we sailed out and away on the next stage of our treasure hunt.

*   *   *

Every day up till now the wind blew steadily from the north —just what we required; but that day the wind died completely. We tacked back and forth, finally anchoring at our usual spot, as a couple of days would not matter and I wanted a good start. Our aim was to pass north of the Cape Verde Islands.

Hugh did not mind, as he had some contacts ashore. Another day passed—this time the wind blew from the west, the wrong direction for a change, and in any case still too light to make it worth while casting off.

"Let's do some fishing. If we get enough we can salt them down for emergency," said Jill.

This seemed a good idea. I also wanted to try out the self-steering in the light airs. Off we ghosted across the bay, me fiddling with the ratio drive on the steering, Hugh throwing buckets of water over himself. It was hot and still—not the kind of day for fishing; but spotting some seagulls diving in the water a few yards from the breakwater, Jill started to throw in our two trailing lines. One was fitted with a miniature paravane which took the brightly revolving hook with its shiny lure down to where, we hoped, the big ones were. The other was a tiny thing, but being on a large big-game reel and rod, any capture could be played out in the accepted manner.

"Nonsense!" said Hugh. "You'd be better employed scrubbing out the galley. You'll get nought in this filthy water."

"I've got one! Oh, he's gone!" said Jill in the same breath. I looked at her line. The hook was gone and she was cut where the line had caught her finger.

"Probably caught the bottom!" was Hugh's only comment. Then a tremendous tug on the paravane line—another hook gone.

"Whatever they are, they're big," I said, and getting a plastic float, attached it to the end of the line. "If you can't hold it, Jill, throw the buoy over the side and we will pick it up when the fish is tired."

Meanwhile, with a whirring scream the line ran out on the rod. I was not taking any chances; we had dropped sails long ago and were on the engine, but I cut that and let the *Charon* lose way. Slowly I wound in the line. Hugh was waiting with the gaff, and with an expert flick of the wrist he tossed the fish into the cockpit. It went mad, and soon blood flecked the whole cockpit: a swift blow on the head with a mallet soon put a stop to it and we examined our catch. About ten pounds, it looked like a cross between a tuna and a mackerel, but there was no time to admire it, the paravane jerked and Jill let it go with the buoy.

As we turned back to it, another fish bit on the first line. And so it went on until we had five beautiful fish, but lost more hooks on the paravane. Whatever size fish were attacking the school from below, we did not find out—but they were certainly huge. Fish fillets were sizzling in the galley, and I took this opportunity to tell Hugh that the dozen whisky bottles aboard were for him, while we would content ourselves with the two-gallon jar of red wine.

"Now that's right good thinking!" Hugh grinned. "Maybe we should have a dram now to celebrate the occasion!"

And so it soon happened that we were all sitting round the cockpit having a drink, while Jill cast an occasional glance at the stove.

We had anchored in a little bay near Cape Vert; the water was oily calm and the light was falling when we saw the tiny canoe coming in fast under sail—if one could call it a sail—a kind of grey-looking sheet tied at each corner, one end fastened to a short pole. As it came closer we saw that the speed was partly explained by the dexterous use of a paddle. These boats were common around Dakar, built like boxes which seemed fitted on to long curved keels. Clumsy and amateur looking, they seemed to have solved the waterline length theory of speed to a nicety; it was nothing unusual to see one eight or ten miles out and, depending on the size, carrying up to twelve fishermen. This canoe had only one passenger; an old man, who waved as he passed, then threw overboard a rock on a rope as he came into shallow water.

"Looks as if we have company for the night," Jill said as she served the fish with tomato, egg plant and green peppers sprinkled with lime juice.

We had an early night, and light was only just beginning to make itself felt the next day when I heard Hugh hard at it on deck. Not wanting to appear slothful, I pretended to be doing something to the engine when he came down—but he was not fooled. Jill made coffee, which went very well with her first attempt at making Scotch pancakes in Hugh's honour.

I went up on deck and was looking about me when I noticed our fisherman of the night before. He was anchored fifty yards away, happily pulling in some small silver fish one after the other.

It was about forty feet deep, shelving rapidly, with the bay wide open to the sea. Jill passed up the garbage bucket which I emptied into the drink without another thought. The pieces of cooked fish, and bits of paper all floated down through the clear water.

An empty can of Watney's beer which had fallen out on the deck rolled, and I picked it up and was about to cast it after the rest when the old man, who was watching out of the corner of his eye, called out something and mimed that he would appreciate the can. I waved back, and with all my strength threw it in his direction. I hit the water maybe five yards from his boat and bobbed on its side drifting towards shore.

As it came closer to the canoe it started to fill, slowly sinking, base down, as the old boy tried in vain to reach it. Then, hooking up his loincloth—or whatever covered the lower part of his body—and throwing off some kind of robe, he lowered himself into the water and reached for the can.

Something caught my eye, and looking hard I saw a large shadow pass swiftly at an angle towards the scene. I leapt into the saloon and grabbed the shotgun, always kept loaded ready for intruders, and back in the cockpit fired a shot into the water. It could not harm the shark, of course, but the sound transmitted through water might scare him. Also the old man would be warned. But the old man somehow had sensed something wrong, perhaps from my sudden disappearance. He had abandoned the can and was holding the gunnels of his boat, about to climb in. The shadow was nowhere to be seen;

it had passed underneath the canoe or shot out to sea. I breathed a sigh of relief.

"What's up?" Jill called in a puzzled tone from below, while I saw Hugh with a set look on his face trying to get the anti-tank rifle up through the forward hatch. Hugh obviously thought that some kind of attack was imminent, and was being practical. I started to laugh, then the old man suddenly rose in the air. There was a kind of flurry, and somehow he was back in the water, his two hands still holding the sides. His face turned towards us, no sound came from his lips, but his teeth showed in a twisted grimace. Round him the water turned red; it circled out from him, and it was obvious the shark had got him.

I snatched the spear-gun, jumped into the dinghy and cast off, rowing frantically towards the victim, thinking I might get him before he let go and sank, or before the shark might have another try. I heard Hugh calling something but was too intent on my task to take note. I almost reached the man. His mouth was open, his eyes dilated, then something struck him, twisted him, his hands still grasping like talons, and pulled him under the water.

As he went, I tried to grab his hair, lost my balance, and the dinghy tipped right over. I came up very quickly, righted it, and threw myself back in record time.

The bay was calm as if nothing had happened.

Hugh standing by the rifle and Jill with a hand over her mouth, both as if frozen, looked out of character with the sun and the waves breaking on the peaceful shore. I paddled back. The harpoon gun had gone below, and one oar was floating towards the sand where it could be recovered later.

"What's happening?" Jill asked, still puzzled by the excitement.

"I'm sorry, but the old fisherman has been taken by a shark," was all I could tell her. Then I saw her look. The dinghy was still a quarter full with water. It was pink.

I felt a little sick myself, and as Hugh and I lifted the boat and tipped the water out, the blood spread around the stern like some kind of marker dye.

What now, I wondered. Should we sail back to Dakar and report the attack? We talked about it in the saloon.

After a long time, I decided. "First, if we do go back to Dakar, who will be in a position to do anything—except that we will be held up by red-tape for the next three months. The old chap probably has no relatives, because if he had he would hardly be alone. These canoes nearly always have two or more, seldom one. Best seems to leave the canoe at anchor, and place a note under one of the stones inside."

It was agreed, and I typed a note as follows: *The old man who used this canoe was taken by a shark and killed at 0900 hrs. on Tuesday 22nd March 1967. Witnesses British yacht* Charon. This was followed by a statement that I would be only too willing to answer further queries if so required.

Hugh went below and busied himself with lashing the anti-tank rifle back on the forward bunk, while I washed out the dinghy.

I then went over to the boat and left the note near the little silver fish and two spare fishing lines, a bottle of water and half a piece of bread half-covered by a blue-grey robe that were the only pathetic remains.

Later, with Hugh standing by, I dived for the spear-gun. We had two more on board, but as part of our future diet was to be fish, we could not afford to lose it. However, little did I guess for what purpose this particular gun was to be used in the future.

I was glad to be back on board. We spoke little that day; each busied himself with the task in hand as we slowly cleared land and headed out into the Atlantic.

*   *   *

I had hoped for a north-east wind, but it was not to be. The wind was north—in fact a little west of north—so that instead of leisurely moving along with the wind behind us, we had to go to windward to try and make up a few degrees of latitude.

The sea was heaving with a deep swell, and after a few hours we all had that dizzy feeling which to a lot of people is followed by sea sickness. In our case it just meant discomfort—especially for Jill in the galley.

Our route to Haiti would be almost assuredly with following winds all the way, but only if we passed north of the Cape Verde Islands into the Trades. If we went south, we would probably get into light airs and make an extremely slow passage across the Atlantic.

The fishing line over the side did its job and two ten-pound Atlantic bonito were dragged in after a half-hour's sport with the big-game rod. I filleted them and salted them down. Our stores were ample, but who could know the future?

Two nights later, Hugh and I were on watch. So far no one had put a finger on the helm; the self-steering was doing its job. We did not expect any shipping, but took it in turns to keep watch just the same.

Porpoises began to jump around us in the dark, making the usual peculiar whoosh as they inhaled air and dived again. Hugh, quietly smoking his pipe, smiled and pointed at one playful creature which came up almost on the deck and I went down to get Jill as I knew she liked to see these friendly mammals.

I had often heard that porpoises talk to each other, but always imagined this to be a high frequency sound inaudible to human ears without elaborate apparatus. Then I heard them. Whirry kind of whistles, terminating on a dying note. Jill and I stood enchanted. The fibreglass hull had always acted like some kind of stethoscope magnifying underwater sounds, but never to that extent. The porpoises were obviously swimming just under the keels. Two could be easily distinguished from the others, having a deeper note, and one had a distinctive squeaky tone. Jill rather thought that he was a baby one. I wished that I had a tape recorder with me.

This school must have followed us all the way. Every night they appeared, and played around at intervals. As soon as daylight began to rise, they disappeared altogether.

Everyone fell into the routine that was to be theirs for the rest of the crossing. Jill arranged and re-arranged her stores—no mean feat, as these were scattered throughout the vessel in such a way that she could get her hand on any given thing without having to unlash or unpack unnecessarily.

Breakfast was to be toast and margarine (butter does not keep), coffee with Long-life milk, half a grapefruit while they lasted then canned grapefruit segments, marmalade, Fowler's Old English treacle, Marmite. Lunch—cold salad with tomatoes and onions, fresh fish cutlets or canned kippers, baked beans, or other canned fish. The main meal was in the evening, using sweet potatoes, new potatoes, egg plant, tinned meats, with either rice or red beans. On the night watches, soup or Bovril.

We carried plenty of fruit-juice, and intended to take vitamin tablets daily when the fresh fruit and vegetables ran out. We even had eggs, dipped in paraffin wax, and lean bacon packed in salt layers.

Hugh methodically went through all the ropes—rigging, sails and everything connected with the vessel, checking, greasing, a new whipping here, a splice there.

I checked the sextant for errors and took various sights, fixing our position as we moved closer to the scattered Verde Islands. Of all the wrist-watches on board, Jill's seemed to be the most accurate, which was just as well, as our receiver could not pick up the W.W.V. round-the-clock time signal from Washington. Exact G.M.T. time was vital for accurate navigation.

All was going well and everyone was in fine humour. Hugh was back to his normal two or three words per day. A man of few words was Hugh. I had only heard him unbend two or three times since I met him. Once was on the subject of women; he had been married once, but it had apparently been an unpleasant experience. When reading the Koran later he saw the quotation "All women are evil: lucky is he who finds her in the mildest form," so Hugh had decided that the Moslems knew a thing or two and wandered off to Morocco. A few years there had given him a new outlook on life, but underneath he was still the same dour Scot.

The English were another subject. Lord, how he hated them! Luckily, as an Australian, I did not qualify, in Hugh's eyes, as a descendant of the murderers of Flodden Field—a pretty drastic battle by all accounts, the whole Scottish nobility being slaughtered. I could have sworn that Hugh had been there himself, as he breathed warm whisky in my face, waved an imaginary claymore, with his eyes glittering and his red beard sweeping the ash and cigarette butts out of the saucer on the table. That was only the second time I met him, and I thought him a pretty fierce character as he sat in the Arab café pounding the table, accidentally digging a wiry elbow into our neighbour whose mint-tea spilled on his robes.

The Arabs looked a bunch of real cut-throats, but they seemed to accept Hugh. Later I found out that anyone in trouble—Arab or Christian alike—only had to call on Hugh: even an Englishman.

Hugh had been brought up an orphan in one of the slums of Glasgow, and his youth had been no picnic. Somehow he had escaped and had taken to the sea. An idealist at heart, he had had a spell as a Communist, and as far as I could gather he had spent enough time behind the Iron Curtain to speak passable Russian. He had worked in the Candian outback cutting timber, on oil-fields, in mines; he had been in jail, and once had made enough money to retire, but lost it again, coming back to his first love—the sea.

"Communism, Capitalism, Fascism—all the same! Just systems for living. For those who can lead and organize. The people have to be led. If they weren't, they'd murder each other. I used to think, let's weed the bastards out, what are the rich doing while the poor are starving? But then I soon learnt; give the poor a chance and they do exactly the same thing. It's every man for himself. . . . All I want is peace, somewhere no English people go."

That was Hugh the third time I met him.

Since then I had come across him a couple more times, and I knew that this scraggy, red-haired, ageless Scot was a real friend.

Here he was with me at sea, looking somewhat different, as he had shaved off his flaming beard before leaving for Dakar. He was ready for a treasure hunt, but, I thought, really only in it for the life and calm of the sea. Something had happened to Hugh since I had last seen him. He seemed disillusioned, but I expected that it was only a temporary thing.

On the third day Hugh remarked: "Ay, but she's getting rougher." It was! The morning coffee wouldn't sit on the table. I held the kettle full of boiling water and told Jill to hold the coffee pot while I poured. This I did, returning the kettle to the safety of the gimballed stove, when the ship gave a lurch and slipped sideways. I fell on my face and Jill screamed as the coffee pot overturned. Hugh was at the first-aid box in a flash, holding a 'Terra-Cortril' spray.

Quickly I sprayed Jill's hand and leg where the scalding liquid had fallen. It was a nasty burn.

"Lie down and take it easy. Hugh and I will handle things," I told her, then had a quick look at the chart. We were to pass south of Ilha da Boa Vista in the early afternoon.

Not a very hospitable spot, no port at all, but with northerly winds we could probably come in as close to the south as possible and anchor there for a while. I suggested this to Hugh: "Until we see if Jill is O.K. The trouble is," I mentioned, "you have no papers, so if we go into a port there's bound to be trouble. It's O.K. in Jamaica, but here with the Portuguese we will be held up for months."

Hugh was all for pausing off the island.

Boa Vista is one of the group of fourteen islands in the Verde group, administered by the Portuguese Government. The

---

10 Rough seas in the open ocean.

population is composed mainly of half-castes and negroes going back to the days when the islands were used as a depot and convenient drop-off place for sick slaves. Nothing grows on most of them, and the main export is salt. Usually hidden by a haze, they have to be approached with caution. It was not surprising, therefore, when the island appeared suddenly only about three miles off.

The south-eastern side was better than I had anticipated— one long, unbroken beach nearly four miles long. We approached, and the echo-sounder showed the bottom to be regular and apparently sandy. About half a mile off, in forty feet of water and out of the line of foaming breakers which crashed with a roar on the sand, we dropped the hook. The *Charon* lay almost without motion. We had a quick snack then went to our bunks to catch up on lost sleep.

Jill, so she said, was comfortable the next day, but large blisters were showing and I decided to stay another night before making any further plans. Just as well perhaps, as the wind increased to near gale force, which blew the haze away and the island stood out sharp and clear. A beautiful beach, but no grass, only barren rocky hills, glowing with heat; about a mile from us, close behind the beach, a dozen or so green trees were the only sign of life. Hugh sat in the cockpit with his pipe and thought it was fine.

The second day a fifty-foot fishing boat with a tough-looking bunch on board circled us a few times. I checked the armament and Hugh said: "It might be the Customs—I'll hide in the forward cabin." I saw him unlashing the anti-tank rifle, and almost wished that they might turn out to be pirates. Hugh had a 'thing' about that deadly piece of machinery. I remembered how I had lost most of the skin off my elbows when I fired it for

---

11 Flying above the mast of *Charon of Styx*, with her twin-sail running rig hoisted, is a red-billed tropic bird, whose long white tail feathers look like a marlin spike, to give it the sailors' name of bosun bird.

12 Hugh MacDonald on the helm.

E

practice that time in the Burnham marshes, and I wished him joy of it.

"There's a man in uniform," called Jill from the deck. Sure enough, they made an approach—always a precarious affair when the sea is rolling. Eventually three men managed to get on board, but I waved the rest away and threw their mooring line back at them. Their boat was much too cumbersome to lie alongside us, with its metal faced rubbing bands and no fenders.

The three turned out to be very nice, each drank a whisky and smoked a cigarette, then left without looking over the boat. I wonder what they would have said had they slid the forward cabin panel aside and been faced with Hugh and his 'Cannon'.

"Well, that's that!" Jill said when they had gone. "It looks as if we don't really have to worry about Hugh's papers—no one cares!"

Thinking about it, I realized the truth! Only in England had I ever had a vessel really looked at. In fact, in some ports no one comes on board at all, and if they do, all they want is a drink, a cigarette and a little conversation.

A large vessel anchored for shelter from the N.E. gale that night, proving the Admiralty Pilot to be slightly optimistic in its description of conditions in the Verde Islands as o·6 days per month with wind speed twenty-seven knots or more for March. The ship, presumably intrigued by our small yacht, began to send 'AA' with their signal lamp ('AA' standing for 'Call Up').

"Maybe they want to invite us for dinner, or a drink?" said Jill. She was probably right. But with a full gale blowing and nearly a mile to cover, it would have been inadvisable for us to attempt the crossing with our rubber dinghy. In any case, I had no Morse lamp on board. I tried to reply using a press-on-press-off type of torch, but this only seemed to confuse them. Finally, in desperation, as their lamp kept blinking interminably, I sent 'EZ' ("What is the best time to cross the bar?"). There was a pause; then a frenzied series of flashes came back.

This time I sent 'R' ("The way is off my ship; you may feel your way past me.").

They gave up. They had sailed by the time we got up the next morning, and we shall probably never know what it was all about.

As we came out of the lee of the island, we realized that the sea was not as friendly as it had looked near the beach. Great white-tipped rollers; even with the main well-reefed and a storm sail instead of the jib, we moved at well over six knots. Sailing to windward under these conditions is trying, to say the least; by the morning we were feeling a bit jaded, and Jill's blisters were rubbed raw whenever she moved.

The island of Sa Nicolau loomed ahead. I had charts of the group, but these are not to be taken too seriously, if the warning printed on them is anything to go by. "As this chart is compiled from old and incomplete surveys, it should be used with caution especially in the neighbourhood of Boa Vista, off which many uncharted dangers may exist." This, coupled with another statement to the effect that Boa Vista was actually one and three-quarter miles further east than on the chart, did not encourage me to get too close to any of them.

But it looked as if a stop was indicated. Preguica, the so-called port, looked to be well sheltered from the N.E.

Cautiously I made my approach, with Hugh in the bows keeping a look-out. The sea abated, but the wind still screamed down as we came to the anchorage where a two-masted trading schooner lay snug almost against the rocks.

Noticing a small harbour wall, I decided to have a look at it. As we rolled our way slowly over, a boat shot out with three rowers and a uniformed gentleman, who came alongside and swung aboard. The Customs man spoke English of a sort and said that it was quite safe to enter the harbour.

I felt a bit jittery when I realized that it was just about big enough to swing around between the wall and a very nasty looking rock over which the sea rose and fell about three feet.

Something like ten large rowing boats were occupied going

backwards and forward half a mile to the trading schooner, unloading bags of maize together with large lengths of timber, to be lifted on to the concrete breakwater by a hand-operated derrick. At times the sea passed under the breakwater, which was really only a bridge to the rock at the entrance. This made it necessary for the boat crews to be extremely attentive, or take the risk of being keel-hauled as it were, passing under water through sharp rocks to the other side.

I was all for getting out again, but rowing boats came on all sides, lines were taken, and soon we were moored with a line right across the harbour to a bollard on the other side, two other lines from our stern to the quay, and for good measure I dropped the anchor in the middle.

The Customs chief then came on board with an interpreter whose mother owned a general store (for want of a better word) seven kilometres away in the town of Ribeira Brava. He was only too happy to take us there in his jeep, up the slave-made road through the barren hills. The town was a tiny oasis—perhaps a hundred houses. We stocked up with bananas, oranges, tomatoes, sweet potatoes, Brazilian coffee—half the price of its English counterpart—and even olive oil and some cans of sardines. Then we drove back and loaded our goods on board, feeling very pleased with ourselves.

The fresh water available had to be carried two kilometres over the rocks; ten escudos (about 2s. 6d.) was enough to have two five-gallon cans filled.

We showered and shampooed our hair; Hugh washed his jeans and shirt, and we sat down to a salt fish curry washed down with some Portuguese wine. Hugh stuck to his whisky. "Wine is bad for you," he said sternly. "They even get the juice out of the grape with their feet!"

Jill's burns were healing rather slowly after our short rest, but the wind was gusting and I felt uneasy in our mooring. Hugh shook his head: "If she blows in, 'twill be hard to get out," he said, quite rightly.

We called for help and in no time at all the natives were

casting us off, and we moved out to have a look at the anchorage. The schooner had left earlier and there was plenty of space, but *Charon* rolled alarmingly.

"Let's try the other side of the island, it may be more sheltered," I said. According to the chart, a north-easter should not bother the other side at all. We headed south with the wind behind us.

The gusts coming through the hills were probably force 8 and 9. Just with the storm sail, we raced the few miles to the point and there faced an unpleasant surprise. The wind became dead in our faces, waves washed over the deck, while spray came at us flat along the surface of the water. With the engine at full power we just made headway. It was a case of hugging the coast to avoid the heavy seas, or making for the open and going off.

The vessel was well found; we were stocked up as much as we would ever be, but if we went, Jill was in for a rough time for anything up to forty-eight hours. Bad weather is never pleasant at sea; if sick to start with, it could be absolute hell. Three hours later we made the five miles to Tarrafal, a tiny fishing village with one tree—the only green growth on the whole of that side of the island. The wind seemed to blow stronger, if anything, coming down through the hills in great blasts. A hundred yards from the beach, in about forty feet, I dropped my heaviest anchor and let out the forty fathoms of chain. The spare anchor with its chain and a 150 feet of nylon also went over the side.

Three or four fishing boats were sheltering; I noticed one with three anchors out *and* a long line to a bollard on the beach.

At times, when the wind reached hurricane force, the mainsail had to be doubly lashed down on the boom and the storm sail taken below. I began to wonder if the anchors would hold, but they did, and soon we retired below for a pre-dinner drink. For the first time, we realized that we were all white, covered in salt, as each successive soaking had been dried up by the wind and sun.

The wind was less the next day, but on approaching the lighthouse we were hit by a screaming bundle of water and high pressure air, which laid us nearly flat. I feared for the sails, reefed down as they were; then Hugh came up from below. "She's making water fast," he called.

"Take over, Hugh, and bring her about!" I shouted, and dashed into the saloon.

First things first. I bent down under the galley basin and turned off the sea-cocks to the self-draining cockpit, to the basin, and sea-water pump. Then to the toilet and off with the inlet and outlet. Now all closed; time to look about. First a foot of water sloshing around. Windows next, saloon O.K., forward cabin O.K., toilet—ah! The pane was half out and even as I looked a great onrush of water poured in and threatened to take the plastic glass away altogether. I looked closely; it was not pushed in, but strangely enough pushed out.

Up on deck quickly. Hugh was doing all right heading for calmer waters. I rushed up to the window and pushed it back into its recess. If it had been a wooden boat, I could have hammered a piece of timber across it; but fibreglass is a different proposition. The screws holding the frame were all pulled out; no use pushing them back, they would not hold.

We got back to the anchorage and we had a good look; lucky for us that calm waters were close.

It meant drilling holes right through the frame and fitting bolts from one side to the other, holding both frames with the fibreglass in between. A lesson! As soon as we can we shall have to get more bolts and do *all* the windows. The only place for that would be Port Grande—the largest and most commercial of all the Verde Islands, luckily on our course and not far away.

We wanted reasonable weather. It was worth waiting for if we had to, especially after pumping for two hours and drying out the gear which somehow should not have got wet. Water had found its way under both saloon bunks, cans had to be dried out or they would rust. Most of our perishable stores—

beans, rice, flour etc.—were in plastic containers. It was not tragic—just a bloody nuisance.

Another day passed. The sheltering boats suddenly started their engines and, heaving up their accumulated anchors, putt-putted out to sea. They must know something, I reasoned, as we followed suit. Certainly the weather was not as bad on the point, but still left a lot to be desired.

A few hours later we rolled by in the lee of the uninhabited island of Santa Luzia. It looked sheltered, with a two-mile sandy beach and a few rocks at one end—perhaps good for swimming. Porto Grande would be fine for getting final supplies of water, besides nuts and bolts to make all our windows safe; but Jill required a week for her scars to heal and what could be better than a sheltered bight? Hugh was a bit doubtful and we came in carefully checking the depths; rocks there were, but also large patches of sandy bottom, good holding ground for our anchor.

In twenty-five feet we finally let go. With both anchors down I thought we could sit out a hurricane, and just to show me a gust screamed through the hills, laying us almost flat. But the anchors were well in, and the sea was calmer than it had been before.

Our only problem was going ashore. The wind came from there, sometimes too strong to row against. Once blown out to sea there would be no coming back. Getting all the spare cordage, I made up nearly 600 feet, and with me rowing like a maniac, Hugh let it out until we buoyed the dinghy near the beach. Now all we had to do was pull ourselves ashore and back.

Making a landing was another problem. Every sixth or seventh roller broke with a crash on an uneven reef in four or five feet just short of the sand. The dinghy could be taken in, but it was better to anchor it and swim in. As occasional sharks used the bay, it meant taking care.

Soon we were exploring the uninhabited ruins of a small village. Skeletons of cattle, sheep, and even a mare and her foal, gave the impression that some plague or other disaster had overwhelmed the village a few years before. We gathered limpets and had them grilled with rice and tomatoes—not very good, but all in the cause of science.

I used the left-overs as bait, and to my surprise caught a three-pound sergeant major (a bream-like fish with black and yellow stripes, hence its name), followed almost immediately by a Spanish Grunt (this is not a misprint, but the name of a specie of silver edible fish).

"Wouldn't think there'd be any fish on this sandy bottom," Hugh commented.

The next day I set out early in the dinghy, supposedly to get more bait, but actually with my spear-gun, flippers, mask and all the gear. Just off the beach, as I had surmised in the night, hundreds of coral fish swam back and forth, coming in after every crashing roller to eat any uncovered creature; bigger fish came in to eat the smaller, and so on in the usual way.

I shot several fish to start with, throwing them in the anchored dinghy, then noticing an ominous shape, which was no doubt attracted by the blood, I went inside the reef itself to have a close look at the life there. With crashing surf and bubbling waters, it was not easy to see anything; but under one rock a sight caught my eyes. Antennae wiggling, half a dozen crayfish were peering out from under the ledge. It was rough on my hands—I had forgotten to bring gloves—but when I arrived back on *Charon* it was with six small and one large specimen of the *Palinurus Vulgaris* family.

"Lobsters?" asked Jill. Five minutes in boiling sea-water served cold with freshly made mayonnaise, and they might well have been.

The next few days we had so many of them that I started to make plans for drying the tails. Curried, baked, in tomato sauce or near-raw with fresh lime juice, they seemed the ideal cure for burns; Jill's wounds healed almost without a mark.

It was time to go. The two anchors came up laboriously.

"It's a grand place!" said Hugh, as we slipped away fast with the usual gusts coming at us from out of the hills.

"Tell me, Hugh, what will you do if we get our hands on a ton or two of gold?" I asked him. "It looks to me as if you'd be happy as a hermit somewhere—maybe on an island like this one."

"Ay, but I have a few things to do yet. When it's all finished, I'll go to Cuba. I have a few friends there."

"Cuba? They'll take it all off you."

"And why not? You can't eat gold!"

"There you are," I said to Jill, who was listening. "This Jacobite goes on a treasure hunt, and what do you think he's after?"

"Maybe peace," she said.

Just then the fishing line ran out with a scream. Hugh was at it in a flash. I dropped the main, while Jill kept steering on course with only the storm sail. We had on only a tiny inch-long silvery spoon used in the Channel to catch mackerel, but for some reason always caught huge fish on it. This time it was a dolphin; not the true dolphin which is a mammal, but a member of the fish family erroneously called by that name. Bright blue back and dorsal fin, with golden undersides, these fish are probably the most beautiful in the sea, but they are rarely seen close up and, when caught, lose their colour almost immediately.

Two hours later it tired and was hauled on board. It weighed nearly twenty pounds. We ate that night until we could hardly move, the rest being filleted and hung to dry on the hand-rails, later to be salted down as a useful protein addition for our trip.

We had estimated that we carried basic supplies for six months, allowing for fresh fish, including a percentage salted and dried whenever possible. We washed in salt water and used it for cooking. Jill had managed so far to use up to 50 per cent salt water in the rice and beans. I had fabricated a kind of still out of the pressure cooker, and was prepared to manufacture a maximum of a hundred gallons if required.

Jill and I enjoyed our own salt fish, curried or Spanish style in a tomato and garlic sauce. Hugh was not too keen, but believed that the ends justify the means and that keeping alive was more important than the culinary delights of a funereal repast.

Porto Grande, after our deserted beaches and native houses, was a surprise. Three large vessels taking on bunkers, plus endless small boats, and even a large luxury yacht, gave the impression that we had returned to civilization. The officials were friendly and wished to give us a berth alongside the quay.

However, we stayed at anchor where the breeze continually blew. Jill and I rowed ashore to top up our water cans, diesel fuel, fresh fruit and vegetables, and to send the odd letters home.

No more stops after that. Our route was direct to the north of Haiti. The next time *Charon* entered a foreign port she would be heavy, we hoped, not in stores or water, but in bullion, gold preferably, but silver almost certainly.

Five

*"An area littered with the wrecks
of blood-curdling piracy and murder,
stretches to the present day"*

SUNDAY TELEGRAPH August 20th, 1967

As usual, the wind was gusty and the sea rough. We crept round
San Antao—the westernmost island in the Verde group—and
altered course once in the lee to get as much northing as
possible. San Antao was bare, with high sunburnt mountains—
higher than any we had seen before. We had only gone a few
miles when I noticed a valley coming down to the sea, and to
my surprise saw that it was bright green all the way down.

"Bananas, coconuts, sugar cane and quite a few houses,"
said Hugh, looking through the glasses. I was intrigued.

"Why don't we go and have a look? We may even pick up a
few more green tomatoes cheap," Jill called out.

We altered course and anchored just off a black sand beach
with the cliff-like rock towering above us.

I threw in my new fish trap which I had made from chicken
netting purchased in Porto Grande, baiting it with various
slops such as cabbage leaves and banana skins.

I found that by tying the holding rope to the anchor chain
and letting out another few fathoms, the rope and trap were
hidden from prying or thieving eyes and safe from whirling
propellers of possible passing craft.

Jill laughed, remembering my last efforts before the Red Sea
expedition.

"As many as one can eat!" she mimicked.

"We shall see!" I grumbled. I thought that she might have
forgotten my lack of success on that occasion. We rowed ashore
and made our way past the huts to the largest house half-way

75

up the hill. Two ladies invited us in, and in moments little boys and girls were dispatched to get our requirements. What we wanted were tomatoes, green, straight from the bush, and a tree of bananas the same way. Then we could be sure of fruit and tomatoes for at least a month; the ones we purchased previously had been green but ripened almost overnight.

We discovered while we were there that this was the point where tankers picked up their water to take to the large ships bunkering in Porto Grande.

"I can wash my hair, and we can top up before leaving in the morning," Jill suggested.

We went back to *Charon* with twenty pounds of large green tomatoes, the plant smell still about them, and a huge bunch of bananas.

That night a sound woke us up like some kind of primordial monster breathing hard. We leapt up and went on deck where Hugh was already hoisting our anchor light.

"Didn't think we'd need that here," he declared.

I looked around and saw the cause of the noise—a large steam tanker was coming in, apparently for water. It clanged and groaned, dropped an anchor and backed almost on top of the ruined pier where a hose was passed on board. Just as well we did not anchor too close, I thought.

We had no need for our alarm clock that morning, as blowing steam and belching dense black smoke, the tanker passed us on its way back. A quick breakfast and I started to heave up the anchor.

"Lunch!" I called to Jill. In the trap were three large red mullet.

"Very good fish," Hugh commented.

"A miracle," was more Jill's idea.

Luckily for us, we had finished our red mullet as the *Charon* came slowly out of the lee of the island. Lightly grilled on both sides, served with lemon juice, the flesh had the consistency of lobster; it would have been a pity to try and eat it the way we had to eat during the next forty-eight hours.

Back against the bulkhead, feet braced on the bunks, holding on to plates doggedly, it was a tiring business. I found the haggis bouncing on top of the green tomatoes in the forward cabin.

"Hey, Jill," I asked, "what happened to Hugh's birthday on the tenth?"

"I'm waiting for a good calm day. It won't matter too much about the date."

And then the wind suddenly dropped. Maybe the gods had been listening, but I wish they had been less co-operative.

With both genoas set on booms *Charon* looked like an ungainly butterfly, the main reefed down slightly was intended to act as a steadying sail, but there was so little breeze that it did not act as anything at all. We barely averaged three knots instead of our expected five to six.

Jill was happy. Like a Christmas pudding, the haggis was being simmered—or whatever one does to haggis. I had scraped off the fuzz and green mould, throwing it over the side to the amazement of the three black and white striped pilot fish which had transferred to us after two killer whales had passed too close—one sounding and waving its tail almost in our faces.

The three newcomers had taken up residence just below the stern. Anything thrown over the side was inspected by one or the other, then a quick dart and back under. Whether they ever managed to grab a morsel or two was never very clear as they moved too fast. They were to stick with us through thick and thin.

We sang 'Happy Birthday' that evening as Hugh came into the saloon to join us for dinner.

The whisky bottle, a special malt blend given to me by a friend in London, was waiting on the table. The days were passed when we had to worry about the gear sliding off.

Hugh was surprised—even more so as his birthday, it turned out, was in December!

When Jill dished out the haggis, his astonishment was complete. Nothing to what he was going to experience as he ate it, I thought to myself. But to my great surprise and relief, the haggis turned out to be a first-class dish. I had never had a haggis before. In fact, years ago I firmly believed, like a lot of other people that I have since met, that it was some kind of animal native to Scotland, either with fur or feathers, but I was never very sure about this. Scots keep canny about the whole thing and others do not like to demonstrate their ignorance; the result is that haggis is a mystery to most of the world.

At last I learnt that it was some kind of sausage, large and bulbous, containing oatmeal and the organs of various beasts; in the last aspect it is a mystery indeed, about which it is better not to enquire too closely, at least if one wishes to continue eating it.

It must have been all right. Hugh swallowed it down with gulps of whisky, and asked for more.

"That was good!" he exclaimed over coffee, and I could see that Jill had enhanced her standing in his eyes, even if she was only a woman.

"Do ye ken Robbie Burns' ode to haggis?" he suddenly asked, and without waiting for a reply solemnly proclaimed:

> "Fair fa' your honest sonsie face,
> Great Chieftain o' the Pudding-race!"

It went on for some time, most of it incomprehensible to Jill and I, ending with something about "Gie her a haggis."

We exchanged glances. Haggis is obviously not to be taken lightly. We then moved out with our drinks and sat in the cockpit for some hours watching the reflection of the moon on the flat calm sea. We were still moving, but with only enough wind to keep the self-steering on the job. I lit the hurricane lamp, to allow for the unlikely event of a passing vessel, and we went to bed.

Crossing the Atlantic is not, as many think, a difficult business. With a well-found ship, plenty of food and water, it is largely a matter of routine.

Hugh and I took watches during the night, which meant dozing in the cockpit or on the fore deck, with a sleeping-bag around the shoulders to keep out the cold.

A hurricane lamp attached to the mast in case of unlikely traffic also added as an attraction to the thousands of flying fish. Unfortunately, most bounced off or slid back into the sea; the best catch was three on one night. Lightly fried in olive oil, or grilled, they were a welcome addition to the rations.

Our time signal for navigation purposes was picked up on Radio Senegal at 1 p.m. and 10.15 G.M.T. for the first half of the journey; after this we got B.B.C. news and time signals through the Barbados station at 2000 G.M.T.

At about 11 a.m. each day I took sights of the sun—and the moon whenever possible—this together with the usual noon sight for latitude fixed our position fairly exactly. Meanwhile, Hugh would try out different sail plans and trim the sails to suit the conditions. The vessel sailed herself with the wind dead astern using the twin booms and genoas; however, when the wind switched to the quarter, especially a light wind, it took a lot of trimming to keep on course. When the wind increased to over force 7, which it did for several days, we sailed under the jib only; trying to set a steadying sail on the main just did not work.

Jill was usually kept busy cooking meals or making bread with Scoffa flour and water—the easiest thing in the world and no one should take on a long yacht voyage without the stuff. Her use of sea water in cooking worried Hugh; he was inclined to regard it as some kind of undiluted poison.

Two large dolphin fish, one on each bow, escorted us across, dashing occasionally ahead to swallow up large quantities of flying fish. Efforts to catch one for the pot failed, but almost worked one day when I used a large flying fish as bait. I tossed it in front of one of them, whereupon he threw himself at it and it disappeared in one gulp, hooks and all, the line parting with a snap. As we did not get another flying fish, I had no opportunity to have another try with a heavier line.

Three birds, large white exotic creatures with orange beaks, almond eyes and two long trailing tail feathers, also came all the way over. Calling on us at dawn each morning and making as if to land, their high-pitched bat-like cries, overriding any other sound. Whether they flew all night or rested on the water, catching us up again in the morning, remained a puzzle.

After ten days or so, we found that we had time for reading and began to go through our collection; that and listening to the B.B.C. news became our chief source of amusement. One has to get away from civilization to appreciate the sick humour of a puzzled world—led by pompous asses, out-vying each other with their bombastic statements, like orang-outangs in the mating season.

One morning, for instance, the new Greek Government, which had given a promise the night before of a new Democratic Constitution designed to improve the standard of living, announced that it had outlawed over 250 trade unions and cultural associations. Meanwhile, Bertrand Russell and Jean-Paul Sartre, discussing their forthcoming War Crimes Tribunal, to be held in Sweden, in reference to the Vietnamese war wiped off the U.S. Secretary of State, Dean Rusk, as being only a 'mediocre functionary of the United States War Department', bringing back the retort from that worthy that Bertrand Russell was of no account, as having the mind of a four-year-old while Sartre was only a Communist anyway.

President Johnson was said to be making a decision to step up the Vietnamese war by increasing the number of troops from 450,000 to 650,000. Casualities of 100 U.S. troops, as against 1,000 Vietcongs, was said to be a satisfactory 'kill ratio'. Loud protests from Madame Nehru, unexpectedly against the proposed International Nuclear Treaty to ban the

---

13 Jill searching the sea bed for the daily food supply.
14 She surfaces with fifteen pounds of lobster meat caught with her gloved hand.

use of atomic bombs. And last, but not least, above all this plotting on uneasy earth, man's latest achievement was sitting like a happy sand-boy on the moon, 'bleeping' out great masses of data, preparing the way for a triumphant occupation. God help any life on the moon if man gets his paws on it!

"The sea's the only place left," said Hugh with conviction. We agreed with him. But a few nights later we learnt that even the vast ocean is no longer safe from prying eyes.

It was a very dark night, overcast and no moon. We had been sitting in the saloon and had not bothered to light the hurricane lamp, while Hugh recited long passages from Robbie Burns which, I must say, sounded very nice with all the rolling 'r's'—but what it was about I could not make out.

"Well, it's my turn tonight," Hugh finally said, and went to the cockpit; then, almost immediately: "There's a ship ahead."

I joined him. Sure enough, a mile or so away, a large white light shone brightly. I looked through the binoculars, a dark shape below the light, low on the water, no green or red navigation lights.

It seemed to be moving fairly fast.

I switched on our navigation lights, which we normally did not use, to conserve the battery, and at the same time made sure that the engine was ready to start. I was taking no chances of being run down by a vessel on automatic steering while the look-out was having a cup of tea below—a thing which once happened to a friend of mine.

To our surprise, the bright light was almost immediately extinguished. Whoever it was did not want to be seen, and the next half-hour felt eerie—as if we were under observation from something in the darkness. We all felt it strongly.

What was it? A Polaris submarine with its deadly load, or maybe a flying saucer? One thing was certain: we would never know.

---

15 Ted sets off, on a raft, the slow fuse which will fire the explosive charges to blast coral from the wreck of *La Nuestra Senora de la Concepcion*.

F

Our plan was to sail directly to the Silver Reef, north of Haiti, where our wreck lay waiting for us. Unfortunately, when inspecting the self-steering rudder, I noticed that it was vibrating badly, and two of the holding bolts had sheared off; then Hugh reported that one of the castings on the alloy booms had fractured. So much for the latest in alloys and stainless steel. The holding screws had fallen out, and one end of a boom was badly bent. Made to take a fantastic strain in the middle, the designers must have forgotten that the end fittings also need to be up to it. I was reminded of a yacht at the last Boat Show, with rigging of five tons breaking strain, but bottle screws tested only to two tons.

As *Charon* was built of fibreglass, with an aluminium alloy mast, and stainless steel rigging, I had wanted to keep all extra gear in like materials; but it would have been cheaper and better to stick to the old-fashioned galvanized fittings, and to have taken a few stout poles to be cut and fitted as booms when required.

Hugh said: "Give me a wooden boat every time; with a kit of tools, you could sail round the world till doomsday."

He was only too glad to have his theories vindicated; and we had already debated for long hours on modern methods as against traditional boat building.

He had a point there; the weakness lay in the fact that modern materials lent themselves too readily for amateur use. Used as it should be, weight for weight and cost against cost, stainless steel is superior to galvanized, fibreglass to wood, alluminium alloy to heavy spars—but only if it is first-class stuff, intelligently used. I had this in *Charon*.

A thirty-year-old yacht kept in reasonable condition will last another thirty; but a modern vessel slapped together as they so often are today will look wonderful for a few months and then slowly fall apart. As fibreglass is for ever, the unfortunate yachtsman can at least be certain of a fine coffin.

We heaved to, and using the coil of wire taken just for such an emergency, repaired the four boom ends as best as we could.

The bolts on the self-steering rudder were something else. It seemed impossible that they should have fractured, being five-eighths inch thick. Jill remembered a bumping during the night, as if we had gone aground. I had been awakened by a strange noise myself, but had not placed it as neatly, thinking we had hit some floating object.

I put on my wet suit, and with the mask and flippers went over the stern to have a closer look.

Although the *Charon* had been fully anti-fouled before being launched from the *Thackeray* in Dakar, hundreds of brightly coloured barnacles were already well away underneath the stern, some nearly an inch long.

The propeller was almost hidden by a large bunch of sargasso weed, patches of which we had been ploughing through since half-way over. I thought I had better have I look at the engine intake, when I suddenly realized that a large fish was calmly parked neatly between the two keels. The tail was facing me, and it looked very much like a shark. I decided that the rudder could be repaired from the surface after all, and swiftly returned to the deck.

"That explains it," said Hugh, "he's been scraping his hide on the hull and maybe fouled the rudder."

"Hell! That's why we have those pilot fish—they must be his!" I looked around my store of spares and found, to my chagrin, that they were mostly under water. Somehow, water had infiltrated under the stern bunks; injectors, filters, and bearings were ruined. Nuts and bolts, however, were unaffected; none were large enough, but O.K. for length.

Hanging over the sides, with Hugh holding my ankles, I tightened the rudder together, hoping that Jericho—as Jill had already baptized our new razor-toothed travelling companion—would not decide to remove my best spanner together with a few fingers.

Ready to continue not a moment too soon, as the rolling was making us definitely dizzy—we hoisted the sails and relaxed over a cup of tea laced, on Hugh's advice, with whisky.

"That settles it!" I told them, "we don't want to continue as we are. As it is, I'll have to tighten those nuts at least three times every day, and Jericho is bound to have a crack sooner or later. Hanging over the stern is no joke, anyway; the booms won't last long as they are, and if there's an unexpected blow we'll have them both around our ears like a pair of wet socks. I suggest that we get behind one of the islands for a couple of days and do our repairs in peace."

Hugh agreed, while Jill was all for seeking new territory.

I looked at the chart. We were on the 18th latitude. If we continued straight on we would reach Barbuda, one of the lesser known Antilles; it was once a privately owned island whose owners had anticipated Hitler several years by breeding selected slaves which were then sold at top prices. The net result of this is that the Barbudans are today considered the best-looking natives in the Caribbean.

I did not have the Admiralty Pilot for the area, or anything but a general chart of the Caribbean; but with care that was no problem. So a few days later we made a cautious approach to the low-lying island, barely perceiving it at three miles with fierce squalls blotting out the landscape, and drenching us with ice-cold rain as we battled with the genoas and booms, changing sail constantly to try and anticipate the next move of the wind.

I withdrew the log and immediately put out two fishing lines. The large hook went with a twang and fifty yards of eighty-pound line, while the tiny spoon, an inch and a quarter long, with its equally tiny three-pronged hook on a big-game reel and rod, whistled out until I slowed it down; fifteen minutes later a twelve-pound albacore lay gasping its last in the cockpit.

The lesson here is clearly to stock up with at least a dozen of these spoons, sold in Falmouth for about ninepence each, instead of using expensive gear, which unfortunately seems to attract large monsters who take all before them. If a fish is carefully played, it can be landed by tackle originally designed for small mackerel.

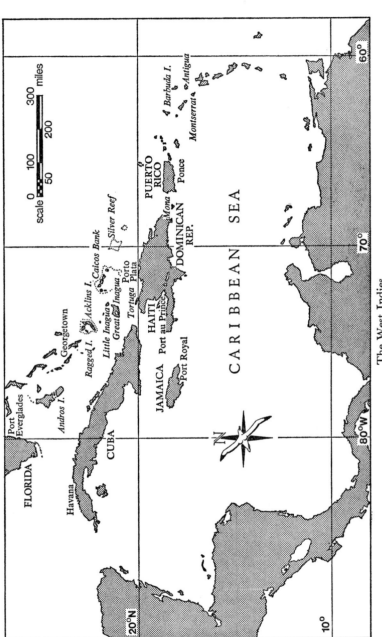

The West Indies

But my problems were over as far as large tackle was concerned. I had lost the lot, whereas the tiny spoon was now credited, according to my log, with 112 pounds of fish, including tuna, bonito, and dolphin.

We anchored in fifteen feet of water, unfortunately opaque, with fine sand, a few yards off a five- or six-mile beach; then we rigged up the awning—a cunning device fitted with a funnel-like aperture—and as a squall hit us soon, had a few extra gallons of water, tasting slightly of new canvas, but palatable just the same.

I cautiously went over the side to see if the mysterious Mr Jericho was still with us. He was not, neither were the pilot fish, our two escorting dolphins, nor the three birds. The next day we went ashore, taking the shotgun, but saw only small birds and a pelican—a clumsy, bald-headed creature which dived into the water in a most ridiculous manner.

The township of Codrington lay over an inland lagoon, nearly as large as the island itself. Then with the drill, wire, hacksaw, and hammer, the booms were soon serviceable again; the rudder became, if anything, stronger than before. However, Hugh was unsatisfied. "If yonder booms were proper spars, they'd now be as good as new: but this new-fangled stuff will all burst asunder if we get a gale of wind."

"We shall see," I said, finally discovering what made the echo sounder give ten different depths at once.

"Use the lead, man! That bloody thing is no use to man or beast!"

Hugh sure had a point. I must admit that he was slowly converting me, and later I found myself using a lead block on a new length of line which was slower, but at least accurate.

Well rested, we decided to sail on the next morning. Our last evening was spent with the plankton net and a home-made bamboo framework, resulting in two or three pounds of a kind of whitebait. Using the underwater spotlight over the side, we waited until they were thick over the net, then whoosh! up she came—baby fish, halfbeaks (a kind of miniature garfish with a tiny lure at the end of its nose, almost invisible), prawns, baby eels, and God knows what else.

It made a very tasty fry-up for breakfast the next morning. Hugh unbent enough to taste it after his usual porridge, which he had converted me into eating, liberally covered with Fowlers Old English treacle, instead of salt, and swimming in the Long-life milk which was still holding out—a remarkable feat since we had loaded it at Tower Bridge four months before.

Jill made a new list of our rations, showing that we could last another four months if we caught rain water.

Radio Antilles, based on Monserrat Island, gave an encouraging forecast of moderate breeze, which turned out to be a near gale, and a time signal two minutes behind the B.B.C. Time does not matter very much in the Caribbean. It would have meant nothing to us either, but for the navigation in which a few seconds can mean several miles.

One thing was becoming fairly evident; we were going to have trouble diving on the Silver Reef with the kind of weather we had been having. A big swell, and wind to thirty knots is not exactly suitable for anchoring close to unsheltered reefs. It we waited much longer we would clash with the hurricane season officially starting in June; and what of the other expeditions?

The weather would bother them, too, but being faster they could always run for shelter to the mainland, whereas we would be stuck on the reef.

"Well, we always have the survival kit," laughed Jill.

The survival kit was my idea, Hugh did not go much on it, but having been adrift three times in my life without food or water, I was not taking another chance. In a service kit-bag, lashed permanently to the Avon rubber dinghy when at sea, was a solar still for making fresh water, a full gallon container, fishing gear, awning to protect us from the sun, Bovril, bully-beef, and vitamin pills, together with the harpoon gun with mask and flippers. Three persons would be able to keep alive for some weeks if adrift.

The only thing lacking was whisky for medicinal purposes, but I was pretty certain that Hugh would never abandon ship without some of his supply.

"It's no use worrying about diving conditions now—we'll have to play it as it goes," I told them.

As I cunningly attached the night's catch—a large flying-fish —to one of the shark hooks which realistically bounced on the water behind us, a short-sighted dolphin mistook it for a live specimen and with spectacular leaps tried to get off; but it was not his day and I slowly pulled him in.

Four feet five inches long—the largest catch so far—it meant enough salted fish to last a couple of weeks.

Hugh shook his head. "It's an unlucky fish," he said.

"Now Hugh, not a dolphin fish; you're thinking of the mammal," Jill told him, but there was no changing Hugh when he had a conviction.

I am not superstitious, but when the wind rose that night and the sea got bigger and bigger, I began to think of Hugh's remark; and when about midnight we were hit full astern with what looked like Niagara Falls, and I heard a loud report—a noise I had not heard before—I looked at Hugh and went over the *Charon* looking for trouble. The jib, all that we had up at that moment, seemed fine. All the rigging was sound.

"She's not steering!" called Hugh.

He unlashed the self-steering and took over, quickly bringing her round, back on course.

"That's funny—it's the first time the self-steering has done that," I thought, and went aft to have a look at it. It seemed O.K. We tried to set her back on self-steering, but somehow the vessel veered off when least expected. I had another look and saw with shock that the rudder, which at first looked perfectly normal, was sheered off completely about five inches below the water.

Hugh was not visibly affected. "We'll just have to stear her by hand," was his only comment.

I did not agree. We had fitted the self-steering to relieve the strain of steering and to give us all time to do other things; to have it out of commission seemed unthinkable.

"It only means getting a piece of suitable planking. I can knock another rudder together in half a day," I said to Jill, who had just come up to see what was wrong.

We were south of Puerto Rico; the port of Ponce was only a few miles away.

Hugh was not happy with this. "I've been to Puerto Rico before. The best thing when you are on a ship there is to stay on it! There's nothing there, mon, but trouble."

Puerto Rico sounded an uneasy place. Alongside it is the Dominican Republic, where revolution had broken out some months before; Cuba, not far away, with its unfriendly habit of landing agitators here and there; finally, and probably the worst of the lot, the Haiti Republic, with its Satanist followers. To arrive without previous arrangement seemed unwise.

We talked around it for a while, and I finally decided to go in, but Hugh would have none of it.

"What about landing me on Los Muertos? There is a good lee there, and you can pick me up on the way out," he said. Hugh's idea at first sounded a little far-fetched, but it was only a half-dozen miles out of Port Ponce, with a lighthouse on it marked as unattended. But why not? We had two walkie-talkies, good for about ten miles across water.

"It'll be grand to stretch my legs," Hugh was saying.

With half a dozen tins of bully-beef, a few tomatoes, and a supply of whisky, I left him on the rocks near a broken-down looking jetty.

"I think he's looking forward to the fishing," Jill laughed, and added, "Hugh's a bit of a hermit anyway."

"It's his business. There's no reason for him to get mixed up with civilization if he doesn't wish to," I said, and concentrated on steering down the buoyed channel. We anchored near the Coastguards, with our yellow flag flying—as required by international regulations for vessels arriving from a foreign port. Usually a pilot vessel comes out with officials—the port doctor,

Customs and immigration. They smile, have a drink, a few forms are signed and that's that. But here, no one showed any sign of life.

After a leisurely breakfast, a wash and general brush-up, there was still no movement from anywhere.

"Better go to the Coastguards and get things moving," I told Jill as we boarded the dinghy and rowed ashore. The Coastguards were very friendly. "We will ring the Customs," they said.

A few minutes later I was asked to go to the telephone. "Do you know that you are breaking the law?" a voice asked. "You have to stay on board until the doctor comes. After he has seen you, then you come and see us."

"Fine," I replied. "And when do you think that the doctor will call?"

"You have to phone him yourself," the voice answered surprisingly.

"But if I am not allowed ashore, how can I phone him?" I wanted to know.

"You must go back on board immediately," was the stern reply.

"Well, that's certainly Kafkaesque, or maybe like 'Catch 22'," I commented, rowing back to the *Charon*.

Then I remembered that the voice had mentioned a yacht club.

"That must be the place on the right as we came in," Jill said. No sooner was the hook well laid than I rowed ashore to the club. In the bar were a few men speaking Spanish. An American yachtsman came over. "Just arrived?" he asked. I told him of our experiences so far. "That's nothing. I'm an American, and it took me two days to clear," he said laughing. "The best thing for you to do is phone the doctor; that's the hardest one to get. After you have seen him, it's a pushover."

I needed a dime for this, which he generously lent me. After a half-hour in the bar trying to get the number, I dialled as instructed.

"Coastguards," a voice answered.

"Look, I am trying to get the doctor. I just arrived a few hours ago. Have you his number?"

A few minutes went by and this was given. I had to borrow another dime. The voice answered: "Customs here."

"Oh, not again! Look, I am the yacht which just arrived. How can I get a doctor?"

"It's up to you to get the doctor yourself, and you are not allowed ashore until he has seen you," replied the voice.

More arguments. Eventually the voice agreed to contact the doctor himself as a great favour.

At 6 p.m. that night I came ashore again. This time I was lucky. The club secretary, back in harness, tracked down the doctor and said: "He'll be here at 7.30 p.m. Now I'll phone the Customs and tell them you'll see them in the morning. They'll come tonight, of course, if you want them to, but I would not advise it as they'll charge overtime—about seventy-five dollars."

"Seventy-five dollars!" I groaned.

About 8 that night, the doctor came, and a bit of comedy ensued. He said that I was not allowed ashore.

"But how would you go out to my yacht, if I can't go ashore to pick you up?"

The same old story! Eventually, all the papers were in order, the itinerary and dates since leaving England all entered down carefully. He was put out slightly by my not having a 'Deratarization Certificate', but I promised to get one—with no intention, of course, of doing so. In all my yachting years I have never seen any reason for a statuary declaration to the effect that my yacht was free from rats.

"Well, at least we'll be able to have a look round tomorrow," I told Jill.

Early next morning the Customs man was there, but our rubber dinghy was something he had never seen before. Another impasse! Finally Bill, the owner of the American yacht, came to the rescue again by lending his dinghy. We no sooner composed ourselves to the task of filling in forms, than loud whistling was heard from the shore. Another Customs man was arguing with the manager of the yacht club.

"He is not allowed ashore; that man will be fined a hundred dollars." Meaning me. I had apparently been seen rowing across to the club house.

The sight of our visitor in his uniform sticking his head out of the cockpit settled the debate. Finally, the official asked us to call at the Customs House to fill in the 'Declaration'. We walked the two miles to the office, and found that we were expected to have brought *all* the ship's papers, notwithstanding the fact that they had already been well and truly perused by our morning visitor.

More walking. By lunchtime we were clear, free to go about three miles further on to do our shopping. But all we had was sterling as the bank at the port would not change it. The bank in Ponce Town would not change less than £50—and at a very low rate of exchange.

However, our travel cheques were valid. Without them we would have been well and truly in the soup, especially as the Customs required $1.50 for entry, plus another $1.50 for a clearance before sailing. Several self-service stores were available, selling mostly American goods at about 30 per cent more than in the U.S.A., so we were informed.

We did our purchasing, and I obtained the heavy bolts needed for the new rudder. Marine-ply was not available in the size required, so I decided to return and ask the club manager's advice. Jimmy Vidal—for that was his name—took me to the back of the yacht club, where large stacks of assorted planking lay.

"Take what you wish," he said. No charge. That's hospitality! I took my tools ashore and started work. But this time I was not thinking of making just one; I decided to make a spare rudder as well. No more hold-ups. When at 8 p.m. that evening I called Hugh on the walkie-talkie, as previously arranged, he sounded amused about something.

"All fine, mon. It's the first time I've seen a man drink with a goat."

That had been his only reply to my brief message.

"A man drinking with a goat? What do you think he means?" I asked Jill.

"Maybe he's got a touch of the sun!"

"Hugh? A touch of the sun? Never in your life! He must be on to something, but what is it?"

I was puzzled. Leaving Hugh for a few days on his own on a deserted island was his own choice after all; but what was this about drinking with goats?

Later, by chance, I overheard Jimmy Vidal talking to a young American yachting couple.

It seemed that there was a house on the island which a rich Puerto Rican had built after being smashed up in an air crash and partly crippled. So many of his friends called on him in their yachts, up to twenty-five boat-loads in a week, that he had started a club called 'Los Muertos Island Pirate Club'. His interests included a rum distillery, so he even had a special rum, available only on the island—'Isla de Muertos Pirate Rum'. There were wild goats on the island and one tame ram.

What connection existed between Hugh's cryptic statement and these goats eluded me. One thing was evident, the island was not uninhabited as we had thought, and obviously it had a well-stocked bar. Hugh's whisky supply was assured.

As soon as the rudder was fitted and the spare stowed away, we went to Customs and, after some time, finally obtained the required forms to permit us to leave. We sailed just on dusk; the wind was still blowing hard as we punched the head seas towards the island. I gave Hugh a quick call up: "Coming in about one hour's time."

The island had not changed since our last visit, and looked every bit as deserted as before. I rowed quickly ashore, and was relieved to see Hugh quietly waiting.

"What's this about the goat?" I asked as we rowed back.

"All in good time, mon—all in good time." And not a word could I get out of him until we were under way.

We waited impatiently for Hugh to decide the crucial moment for his story. Jill had almost finished cooking the red bean dish with its lavish pieces of smoked ham purchased in Ponce, and simmered for several hours in a Madeira wine sauce of tomatoes, garlic, and olives.

The self-steering was working better than before if anything, probably a miscalculation, as I had guessed the measurements, the original figures not being to hand. We were half-way through our pre-dinner drinks when Hugh took the floor.

"You know, the island wasn't deserted. It must be some kind of home for the insane. I was walking round on the second night, having a stroll like, when I came upon a man talking to a giant of a he-goat. It shook me, I can tell you! He was sitting in a cane chair with a glass in his hand, and blow me if the goat didn't have a glass on the ground in front of it! If the goat saw me he didn't let on—he was too interested in watching the man who filled the glasses. Well, it's hard to believe—but the man gave some kind of a toast and swigged the lot while the goat gave a long suck at the glass, as if he were born to it. I watched from behind a bush next to the house. No sooner had the man finished one bottle than he staggered off and got another. They must have drunk about three between them before the man mumbled something about going to bed, and reeled into the bush, where he fell down and passed out. The goat stood there for a while, then lurched away and blow me if he didn't keel over drunk as a lord! There they were, like two drunken sailors, I've never seen the like!"

Jill just wouldn't believe it. "A man drinking with a goat! You're pulling our legs."

It sounded crazy, but then the club secretary had talked about a party during which a goat wandered into the house. One of the guests had forthwith shot it; the host went mad and had to be held down, yelling that somebody had shot his best friend. And, come to think if it, he was supposed to have purchased another goat the next day. Maybe that was him.

Jill would not be convinced, and I had my doubts—but Hugh stuck to his story.

*   *   *

About noon the next day we were passing close by Mona Island, in the passage between Puerto Rico and Hispaniola, as it was once called but now made up of the Dominican Republic and Haiti. I noticed several sharks.

"This would be a good place for shark repellent experiments, instead of the Red Sea. Pity you are not doing that now instead of looking for treasure," said Jill.

"I wonder," I thought. Sharks had always interested me, I had taken part in experiments, trying out various chemical repellents in the past. It was still at the back of my mind to continue with these after the conclusion of our present quest.

"Listen Hugh, would you mind wasting another day? There's an anchorage just inside the northern side of West Point. We could have a night's rest tonight, and I could do a dive this afternoon just to see what sharks are about."

Hugh had no objections. He knew my interest in sharks, and a chance like this might not be repeated for a long time.

Cruising yachts passing through Mona Passage should not fail to call into Mona Island when the wind is coming from the south. It has a quiet, safe anchorage but if the wind is coming from the north, it is better to go round the point from the settlement.

There is an opening in the reef with a six feet depth, and rather narrow. A post is stuck in a vague way at the entrance. On the beach to the right of a ruined jetty are two yellow triangular leading marks.

Tato, Ramiro, Gordo, Luis and Ponce (pronounced *Pon-say*) are the five stalwart guardians of Mona Island.

Gordo sadly reminisces of lost loves back on the mainland of Puerto Rico, while Ponce shoots fish and catches lobsters in the lagoon, to make delicious Asopao—a local mixture of rice, beans, corn, red peppers and whatever is available that day.

Louis looks like a Cuban outlaw with his khaki cap from service in Korea with the U.S. forces. His ambition is to pay back his mother in some way for her sacrifices in having him educated.

Ramiro did not say much, having just got back from the mainland after hospitalization. He had fallen down an old lavatory cesspit in the dark, and had all his front teeth knocked out.

Tato is something special. He sees a pirate ghost from time to time near the cliff where a fresh water spring is pumped into a tank, to be used as a shower. The ghost used to be on a ship which in the old days lay hidden behind the island, to pounce on any unwary vessel sailing down the passage. The ghost is unhappy in the dark because of the mosquitoes buzzing continually in his ears and hermit crabs crawling over his feet. He says he is a Portuguese and back home things are different.

Mind you, that was 400 years ago; things ought to be slightly different these days.

The five made an entertaining crew. When a hunt is on, which happens every few days when a hunter flies in by air-taxi or private plane (the strip is a rough track with high grass on each side), or when a diving group from a U.S. base arrives on a chartered sloop, a caller by yacht can be sure of a slap-up feed with rum, stewed goat, roast pig—in fact, whatever is available. All visitors are automatically invited. It is well worth a call; only, remember, if you go spear-fishing with Gordo, keep clear—he handles his underwater elephant gun a little flamboyantly.

They invited us to stay as long as we wished, and when asked about sharks appeared vague, but mentioned that it would be

---

16 A shark apparently asleep in the entrance blasted by the charges into the coral.

17 This shark did not turn on its belly before attacking, but its meal had been stunned by a blasting charge.

better if we did not swim at night in the bay as they thought sharks came in for refuse.

I dressed in my wet suit and started to swim to the entrance, with the intention of looking for sharks in deeper waters outside.

I need not have bothered. Right there in about five feet of water, a seven-foot grey nurse casually drifted over and showed no inclination to leave me, nor any fear whatsoever. The water had been crystal clear where we were anchored, but near the entrance it was turgid. In the background another shark started circling.

I returned on board, quite satisfied. Here was a place made for the job, with perfect shelter from the weather and sharks on the doorstep.

"Take a good look at the place, Jill. One of these days we shall be here again."

Jill rather thought she would like to own it.

"Maybe the Puerto Ricans will sell it to you, if our venture comes off. I wouldn't mind a piece of it myself!" Hugh commented.

Little did we realize then that we would remember Hugh's hope in the days to come, and would wish that *La Nuestra Senora de la Concepcion* had chosen a more hospitable place to end her days.

---

18 Some sharks came much too close to the work in progress.

G

Six

"Treasure hunt death riddle"

LONDON EVENING NEWS August 17th, 1967

Maybe it is that I have always been optimistic about the Caribbean; but somehow the weather was not what I remembered on my previous visits. It blew a little too much for comfort, while the rollers were heavy and uncomfortable. It was hard work beating up Mona Pass, instead of going down with the wind on the quarter as everyone else appeared to be doing.

"Where's all this afternoon breeze and warm sun?" asked Jill after our fifth squall that day. The sun was hidden, the sky overcast, while Radio Montserrat in the British Antilles broadcast small craft warnings.

We were making heavy weather of it just off San Dominica, when Hugh noticed an American naval vessel—at least it looked like a naval vessel—altering course for us. A few coloured flags suddenly fluttering in the breeze.

"Wants to know if we want assistance, I think," Hugh hazarded.

I picked up *Reed's Almanac* and glanced at the International Code. It was very nice of them, no doubt, but we were too busy to fiddle around with polite conversation. I gave Jill the flags 'WAY', meaning 'I wish you a pleasant voyage', and said "Stick that up. That should make them happy." Looking at them through the binoculars, I saw the vessel give a violent course alteration. They had certainly taken the hint.

Then I noticed that instead of putting up my flags, Jill had hoisted two yellow flags, one above the other.

"Why didn't you hoist the ones I gave you?" I asked.

"One was already fastened ready to go up, so I put another yellow one with it. They sort of go together, don't you think?"

"Women!" grunted Hugh.

I looked up the Almanac. "There has been unusual mortality among the rats on board my ship," it said. Or, "I have had a case or cases of infectious diseases less than five days ago." That was certainly one to avoid company!

Approaching the diving area, approximately forty miles by thirty of reefs, was tricky work; anchoring was going to be hell, for the swell was too high for my liking. As it was getting dark, I suggested we anchored there, and moved into a more sheltered place the following day in the lee of the main reef.

Hugh, an old seaman, appreciated that what we were doing was foolhardy; we were open to the seas, but if we dragged anchor there were no dangers behind us for a good few miles.

"She'll never drag on that bottom," was Hugh's gloomy prediction. I knew what he meant; with a reef bottom, the anchor would never move, but the chain would snap if caught short round a coral head or under a ledge.

"We are not anchoring here?" asked Jill in surprise.

"I'm sorry, but this is it! Prepare yourself for a rough night!"

Rough it was; no one slept—first a roll one way, then a leap upwards, and crunch, as the cable brought us short. The chain was snagging all right, with the rock sounds transmitted up throughout the boat, but it was a heavy, new chain, and I hoped well capable of taking it. The other anchor was ready just in case.

We were glad to get under way at first light. By the afternoon we were threading our way through the reef itself, the sea was slight, dissipated by the shallows.

My fix of the night before had seemed accurate enough. There was virtually no other way to navigate; all reefs look the same, and it's a nasty moment when the ship glides over a particularly shallow one and you wonder if this is not going to be it.

But it was never as bad as it seemed. The echo-sounder showed ten feet when we appeared to be no more than two or three above a nasty sharp outcrop. The water was not as clear as I would have liked; but it was good enough, and infinitely better than off the coast of England. Another night at anchor. It was not so uncomfortable but more dangerous, as now we could not safely drag; the reefs were all around so the second anchor was kept in readiness, and again little sleep was had all round.

Another two days passed. Our problem was in not being able to go in a straight line to the objective. Somehow we were half a mile away, with a reef between us and it. The fifth day we made it; one geographical feature was obvious—our anchorage was to be in a kind of basin, with reefs in all directions. There was only one sure way out, with another decidedly doubtful one.

With two anchors down, and a long nylon rope and chain with buoys to keep it off the bottom, we were safe as long as the weather remained the normal Trades Winds—not comfortable, but the best we could expect. If a gale blew up at night, we would have to wait for daylight, then make for the high seas—a dangerous undertaking.

"I don't like it!" was Hugh's considered opinion. Neither did I. Nor did Jill, who was to try and cook in a constantly rolling vessel.

"Tomorrow we start work," I decided. "That is, we dive until I feel that we know enough to commence blasting, two weeks maybe, and we'll know if we are on the right track. If it blows, we will have to ride it out at sea. Porto Plata is only seventy-five miles away, but we don't want to go there as it means complications with the authorities if we have anything of value on board. Also, it's bound to be the base for the other expeditions. The less they know about us the better."

We had no idea that the other expedition was *not* at Porto Plata, and had not even left Europe; at that very moment Korganoff was in London trying to sell film rights and raise money for his proposed expedition. As I had forecast, twenty-eight people were too many to keep in line; some backers had quarrelled, and the usual bickering was threatening to make a shambles of the whole thing. Had we been aware of this at the time, it would have made some difference, as we could have called into Porto Plata if only to get a feel of the conditions existing there.

Our food was to consist mainly of fish. The place was swarming with them, but rather than waste time shooting them, I had a long line, it was about fifty yards of floating cord, and every three feet there was a five-foot length of strong gut with a medium hook. Strung out in between this were also five large hooks on steel traces, with twine of eighty pounds breaking strain; this was for the sharks.

There was one thing to be said for the reef: no shortage of shark or barracuda, but we soon found out that the barracuda did not bother about our hooks. They were apparently too well fed on the unfortunate millions of spawning fish, which milled around in large schools in what they thought was the shelter of the shallows. These would become seething cauldrons at dusk, and not the place to stick an unwary foot or hand.

The sharks were different. They liked our bait, or rather as soon as a fish got hooked, a shark would take him—hook, line and all. The mornings would resound to my oaths on discovering the damage. Occasionally a shark would make the mistake of biting at one of the shark hooks. He would be found, usually dead, in a tangled mass of lines.

Some tell you that shark is good eating.

Here and there it is a delicacy. The Japanese adore it.

Shark smells like old socks dipped in ammonia; the flesh is mushy and curiously tasteless. Make fish cakes, and you may get away with it; or salt it and curry it later on. It is hardly a quality fish, however, and some sharks taste worse than others. After the third shark, we decided to give up trying to eat them. the *Charon* reeked with the smell.

I made a point each morning of shooting a grouper, or—if

I felt I had time—three or four spiny lobsters. They took some wriggling out of their holes, and although not equipped with claws, left one's hands, if not using gloves, in a sad state. Mostly they were simply cooked for five minutes or so in boiling sea water. If Jill felt inclined, we cut the tails into chunks and had them deep fried with rice and soya-bean sauce, or sweet and sour in Chinese fashion.

The best fish was a small red one of three-quarters of a pound to a pound, with large eyes, known as a glass-eyed snapper, I doubt if a more succulent fish exists. Perhaps the halibut comes into this class, but very little else; it can be left unscaled, *à la Meunière*, perhaps two minutes on each side. Once on the plate, two or three deft movements and all the bones slip out, the skin opens out and there it is—firm white flesh. Delicious! Easy to catch, it spends its time half asleep during the day under shallow rocks, but shooting the nine or ten required for three hungry people took much too long to do it often.

It also meant using a very weak spear-gun, and hitting it on the head so as not to damage the body. Once, armed with this toy, I found myself facing a large shark. He made a pass at the fish on the end of the spear, then whirled off slamming me into a patch of sea urchins—not the Mediterranean type whose pricks are nothing in comparison, but a smaller-bodied specimen with longer barbs. These barbs hold a poison which stings like hell. The points are so sharp that they go right in to the bone, and one piece in Jill's foot measured an inch. Normally impossible to remove, they have to be left and can still be felt months later. On top of this nastiness, the creatures actually move over towards you and sting apparently from their own volition.

Our wet suits and even thick flippers were not proof against them, so that when investigating a likely depression or ledge in the reef, I made a point of smashing them with a shark prod. This won me a host of small friends, striped light and dark blue with yellow heads, who followed me and as soon as I crushed a sea urchin would dart in to get the exuding egg-like matter. As soon as I moved away, they left the scene of the carnage, keeping closely behind me, and waiting no doubt for yet another feast.

I became their host, possibly a protector. After a few days they joined me as soon as I hit the water; the weak, the discriminated against, following power for its apparent protective image. Willing slaves by force of circumstances, this is often noticeable in nature and sometimes includes the human race.

Hugh did not dive, but his responsibility was great enough; once we were in the water the *Charon* was under his command.

If the wind came up dangerously, which was left to him to judge, he was to fire a burst from the automatic into the water. We would hear it and return. By then he would have the engine going, and have done whatever in his eyes was the seamanlike thing to do.

By night he dozed on deck, while we slept what every diver knows is the complete blackout. Three dives every day, even if no deeper than seventy feet, is a lot of diving. Every drop of the barometer would make Hugh shake his head: "I dinna like it!"

I didn't either. A hell of a place to be—but we would stay until the situation was impossible, or success stared us in the face.

*   *   *

The cannons were still there, unrecognizable for the most part, and of no interest as they hung over the big drop, which was too deep to work. Our treasure, if there was one, had to be on the ledge. Each outcrop had to be studied, each crack examined. Once the decision to blast was made, there would be no turning back—down we would have to go. If we were off the track of the cargo, then all that could be under us would be a few thousand years of rock and coral growth.

The fourth day I shot a barracuda, a good eating fish, easy to cut into slices like a sausage.

He came too close, and as I came out from under the ledge I let him have it right in the middle, not with the baby gun but the compressed air job. His snapping jaws would have made short work of anyone around.

Earlier, I had taken off the reel and substituted a short cord of barely two feet on this spear; a long line is a nuisance in the coral, but with a barracuda it is advisable to keep away.

The next meal was a moray eel, a large one. It kept going into our fish trap, used for catching bait for the long line. In the morning there he would be, bloated, waiting to be let out.

The third time, I remembered the early Romans' fondness for moray; some said that they fed their slaves to them, but I deem it an exaggeration—slaves have always been expensive. I shot it, skinned it—what a job, and presented a foot or so of the thickest part—about six inches wide—to Jill.

But for its resemblance to snake, it proved to have a reasonable flavour and a good texture; there were small bones here and there even in such a large specimen, otherwise it was passable. Hugh did not agree; so to please him morays were barred after that. Later I brought back two large shiny lobsters to make up for his spartan helping of moray.

Then something took a liking to our fish trap—perhaps it was a large shark. Whatever it was obviously charged it repeatedly to get at the fish inside, the result was a flattened heap of chicken wire. I straightened it out, only to have it smashed again. After a few days I gave up.

A large turtle also took an interest in us. Perhaps four feet across, it surfaced every morning near *Charon*, lifted up its ungainly head and looked us over. Once satisfied, it went ahead diving on the small fish, swallowing prodigious quantities and continuing non-stop right throughout the day. Schools of tuna-type fish came in amongst the reef in shoals, attacking anything that moved. Often we were surrounded by them; they seemed puzzled as they milled round in a lost kind of way before getting back into formation and throwing themselves at the small fry.

Barracuda would inspect us as soon as we dived, and a dozen or so would hover before disappearing. Only one stayed put, always just out of range. Whatever I did, he was there; if I stayed too long in one spot he came closer, his group of small attendant fishes, maybe six or so, anxiously changing positions —now above, now below; their living depended on the sweepings from his table. What they did in exchange seemed obscure; perhaps rid him of sea lice or other parasites.

I wondered how he would fare when we started blasting.

*   *   *

It was an unreal sensation out there on the desolate waste of the reefs under the boiling sun and the endless wind—a Dali-like abstract scene.

Half a mile away enormous rollers frothed boisterously as they broke amongst the rocks; by the time they arrived where we were anchored, they were somewhat tamer but still unpredictable.

Not far away a boiler bubbled, showing jagged coral teeth as the disturbed water rose and fell hissing in endless whirlpools.

The world as we knew it had stopped, as if we had stepped aside from the conveyor belt of normal life. Time stood still and thus would remain until, satisfied or not, we decided to climb back on it.

Our labour was purely mechanical; we could only follow what we had to do. Fate would see to the rest.

I wondered idly what Phips had felt 300 years ago. His log entries had been rather cryptic and to the point. No imagination, perhaps? Or was it that his personal feelings were too well under control to insinuate themselves into his official log entries?

March 4th, 1687:
This morning, the wind being at E.S.E. a small breeze, our boats went to work on the wreck and in the evening brought on board 2399 weight of pounds, which we suppose to be of silver, and which we put into 32 bags. This evening the wind freshened and blew indifferent fresh all night.

March 14, 1687:

This day being fair weather, our boats went to the wreck and towards evening they brought on board 41 Sows, 4 Barrs, Dowboyds and other bulloine in all 2542 pounds weight coyns being 622 Pounds.

March 16th, 1687:

This morning the wind Eastly a small breeze, our boats went to the wreck and towards evening brought on board sows, barrs, and other bulloines. Weight 1341 Pounds. Coyne 4559.

He almost sounded bored about it all, and as his entries went on was inclined to skip the description and limit himself to the total weight only.

Three hundred years in this same spot, and what had changed? The sun, the sea, and the sky were all there; time had stood still for them. But if Phips had been here, then surely he must have left some evidence of his stay—perhaps a few empty rum bottles.

I started thinking what could have been jettisoned from his ship, but whatever might have been so long ago, could never be found unless by miracle.

But miracles happen, and as if to prove it, Jill came up with an odd-looking shell she had found in an octopus hole. Examined closely it turned out to be a white clay pipe.

Pipe forms throughout the ages have been carefully recorded by a gentleman known as Adrian Oswald, and are as good a way of dating a wreck in modern times as are the shapes of amphorae in identifying their Greek and Roman counterpart. Jill's find could be bracketed between 1670 and 1710, and thus fitted in perfectly with Phips' visit in 1687.

I tried to visualize the scene of a sailor looking over the side accidentally dropping his favourite pipe into the drink, and letting out a string of resounding Old English oaths. . . . Who knows? Perhaps Phips himself.

Next came heavily-encrusted cannon balls, bar shot, and

finally a wooden rammer, used in those days for packing the gunpowder into the barrel of the cannons. Most of the shaft had been eaten away, and after a few hours in the sun it cracked and broke up, disintegrating into small unrecognizable pieces. What had kept it from being completely eaten up by voracious marine organism was uncertain, but strong saturation of copper salts from a bronze fitting stuck to the side would have helped.

Evidently we were getting warm.

Metal detectors have been well proven on land, due to their development during the wars for removal of mines. But under-water—and especially under rocks and ooze or coral growths—even the most sophisticated equipment cannot be trusted. I had not expected too much from it, but every little helps. The detector we were using was an experimental one employing a revolutionary principle. If it helped us to find gold or silver, then the resulting publicity would help its inventor. It also required testing under practical conditions, and it was going to get it. Once it was accidentally left on the bottom during one of our blasting operations. It was never quite the same after that; the gauge needle used to stick until heavily pounded with a piece of coral.

"Treat it rough, it's expendable," we had been instructed. That it was still working after ten days certainly showed that it was suitable for rugged work. A few more adaptations and I felt that it might have pointed the treasure out to us. Unfor-tunately the inventor was not there to carry out the required modifications on the spot, and my knowledge of electronics has never been brilliant.

Under-water work has its peculiarities. One needs a different set of tools for each separate job. I would have liked to experi-ment with thermic boring for instance. This is a revolutionary method, available through the British Oxygen Company, of cutting through the most obstinate reinforced concrete, rock or any known matter. Oxygen is passed through a tube packed with steel rods. This produces an intense heat when ignited, and applied to the material to be cut, the combination of heat and chemical reaction results in a liquid slag which flows from the cavity being cut.

Unfortunately, this process had not been tried out in seventy-five foot depths, and there were certain problems; the major one was that a thirty-foot yacht like *Charon* was not large enough to carry the oxygen and steel tubes and rods required. Under the circumstances, blasting was our only expedient.

"About time, staying here is tempting fate for sure," was Hugh's comment on the news that explosives were to be used as from the morrow.

Using under-water explosives is not as easy as it sounds; compressed air drilling equipment exists for boring rock ready for the charge, but we had none of these things. A heavy crow-bar and a pick were all we had. These work quite well under water, but it meant long hours and careful survey. If the crack could be opened up, I felt that it would lead to the cave-like area of space left by the decomposed *La Nuestra Senora de la Concepcion*; or, if not her, then it might be another treasure ship.

A crack is a useless spot to place a charge. The blast would only follow the point of least resistance and burst its way probably in both directions, wiping out all the marine occupants and leaving the coral as it was before. I had to drill as deep a hole as possible in the line of the crack, and pack it well with small bags of quick-hardening cement and pieces of rock, after making sure that the submarine blasting gelatine was as protected from water immersion as possible. (This explosive was designed to last several weeks in water, but the danger lay in water seepage into the fuse connection, as the detonator and detonating fuse had already been connected.)

The Cordtex terminated on a wooden board sitting inside a child's inflated dinghy, and was coupled with a short length of smokeless waterproof fuse. After three days of hard work, we reached this state, and lit a fifteen-minute length of fuse. Then we repaired to the *Charon* for a cup of tea with lemon.

As soon as the slow burning fuse had reached the Cordtex, it exploded with a dull crack which resounded throughout the hull of the *Charon* and could not be differentiated from the actual charge as Cordtex fuse detonates at a rate of 7,000 metres per second. The child's dinghy had not been sufficiently protected; half-melted by the blast, it sank almost immediately.

We decided to wait half an hour before going down. The first thing we noticed on submerging was a fast-swimming eight-foot shark, who seemed intent on picking up the half floating fish stunned near the bottom; it was interesting to watch that he moved at them straight and level and not belly side up as often pictured. Once safely in his jaws, he moved off with the fish sticking out, but was back for another almost immediately.

Another smaller shark joined in. It would have been safer to wait until the meal was over, but we were anxious to see the results, so pressed on. A fair-sized piece of coral had been blown aside. I could now crawl underneath to where the ledge terminated at a dead end, but on one side, using the under-water torch, I found that a kind of tunnel continued on.

Another three days passed. Another blast.

*   *   *

Three days is nothing to some people. To a man dying of a particularly vicious cancer, it could be an eternity. Waiting, starving, dying, time has a different value to everyone.

To us it moved at different degrees of speed. Hugh liked peace and quiet. Normally he would have been happy just gazing at the sea, smoking his pipe; but deep down he was a seaman first and peace-lover second. No seaman is happy on a vessel anchored in a dangerous area, surrounded by deadly coral reefs; if the weather decided to change it could become a maelstrom of angry seas from which even a large vessel, let alone a small yacht, could never heave up her anchor and leave unscathed.

To Hugh every day was a gamble greater than the preceding

one, the odds shortening as the seconds ticked by. He had not realized that this could take more than a few days, neither had he been aware that he would be running so late in the year and well into the hurricane season.

"I dinna like it," he would say, shaking his head over the evening meal. "Why don't you be a good lad and lay up in some safe place like Haiti. We could come back in November."

"June too soon, November all over," chanted Jill, quite incorrectly. The doggerel runs: "June, too soon, September, remember, October, all over!"

"I agree with you, Hugh, but only in a way. What about the other two expeditions?" I asked.

"All hot air and bull dust! Whisky talk: you wouldn't get those fine gentlemen within a thousand miles of this place. One week at sea, and it would be for their mothers they'd be calling."

To me three days had been back-breaking hell. Tapping away with the pick and twisting the heavy crowbar into the shot-hole ready for the charge, I usually came back to the boat completely fagged out, and could hardly keep my eyes open. But we were there on the spot, and by God would stay until supplies ran out, or we found gold!

To Jill the three days were a nightmare of trying to make coffee and stopping pots from spilling, with the jerking vessel usually doing its worst first thing at breakfast. She would just have a platter set on the saloon table when a sudden bump would reduce her artistic presentation to a mushy heap on the floor.

It would have made a weaker girl weep.

*   *   *

The oddest thing was that not one of us cared very much whether we got gold or not.

To me it was part of my life away from the nine-to-five rat race. Ever since I began to look around in my life, I had seen the world go from one disaster to another, the most authoritative statements by the most knowledgeable becoming so much dust and hot air.

Finance, of course, is required. If you can pay, no one will bother you; if you can not, you are a bum, and the British Consul will hardly hand you your mail.

Most of the human race are nice people, and with a yacht you meet them.

What was gold to Hugh? His was a mysterious mind, but I do not think he really cared about it, beyond some for pipe tobacco and good whisky, with perhaps a hand-out for some friends.

Jill? Well, Jill is a woman, and it takes a smart man to work out what a woman thinks.

All this probably made us a very unusual treasure-seeking group.

Lao Tse is supposed to have said: "He who claims nothing as his own, can lose nothing that is his."

*   *   *

And so three more days went by, and at the end of it I lit the fuse and set off another blast.

Result—almost the same—an elusive tunnel-like crack ran deep under the coral.

The third time, a sea bird with orange beak and a single long tail feather happened to be flying low as the charge went off. Into the water he fell, perhaps only from shock, but somehow he could not take off again. I picked him up and took him back to the boat, leaving him in the cockpit to recuperate. This bird seemed of the same species as the ones which had followed us all the way across the Atlantic; vicious with fear, his long beak flashed swiftly in the direction of helping hands, so that gloves had to be worn when trying to feed him.

But he would not eat, neither could he fly more than a few yards when cast into the wind, and later he appeared to have forgotten how to swim with his webbed feet. When falling into the water, he flapped helplessly until wet through and in a sinking condition.

"He'll get over it eventually," said Jill.

Meantime we gave him a home in an empty whisky case, and forcibly fed him twice per day with an eye dropper— powdered milk, bread dipped in water, and pieces of freshly- caught fish.

Looking at the result of our last blast, I noticed that the crack was wider and now changed direction deeper under the coral mass. I thought we were near, and only hoped that we did not run out of explosives before we got inside.

That night, as we ate our deep-fried lobster tails with sweet and sour sauce, washed down with the last of the French *Vin Ordinaire*, Hugh was pessimistic. "I was listening to the radio today. They've named the first hurricane of the season. It sounded like *Arlene*, I think. If we get caught here, we've had it! Luckily, it isn't normal for hurricanes to come so far over this way, not this month anyway, but next . . ."

The fourth blasting was spectacular, in that the charge got wet. It did not go off and, while checking it gingerly to find that the connection had seeped water where I had packed it badly, a barracuda attacked and bit my diving knife handle— he was probably more surprised than I was. Strapped to my leg in its black sheath, the pommel must have glinted in the sun. After this, all nickel fittings were painted dark blue with a quick-drying enamel paint that we had on board.

The coral debris was building up, and we spent a couple of days picking it up and dumping it further down. The largest pieces had to be lifted over with air bags. It was hard work.

As another ten days went by, Hugh became more anxious. "We've been lucky with the weather so far, but it can't go on for ever! What are the chances of getting to the end of the tunnel?"

"The tunnel, as you call it, goes right under the main mass; we can't blow the top off, not with what we've got. I can only

---

19 A Mako shark showing the rows of teeth.

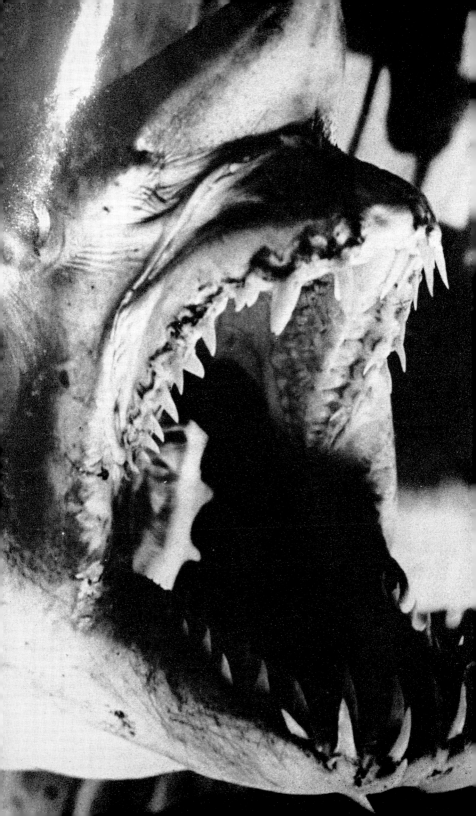

blast about a stick at a time, because I don't want to risk any large lumps collapsing down and sealing it all off."

This was true. What we were working on was a kind of endless crack. I could now go at least twenty feet into it, but what worried me was that so far no wood, metal, or anything except coral rock had been disturbed by the explosion.

*   *   *

Then Jill found an eight-inch bar, covered in coral, which when scraped showed a glinting gold-like colour.

"Is it gold or brass?" Hugh wanted to know.

"Somehow I think it's brass," I told him, "because I've never heard of an ingot this shape. But who cares? The main thing is that it is part of a ship's accoutrement and for it to be under there means that we must be on the right track."

"Isn't there some kind of test we can do?" Jill wanted to know.

But I had not thought of taking some acid along, and the last thing I had thought of was to have doubts like this. If coins had a golden look, surely they would be gold. Here we were faced with an anomaly.

"What would a short length of brass be doing on a Spanish vessel over 400 years ago? Or why should a gold bar be eight inches long by an inch and a quarter diameter, when these were normally flat ingots stamped with the name of the vessel or with the King's coat-of-arms?" asked Hugh.

"The bank will soon tell us," Jill told him.

The next day, another bar turned up. It weighed heavy, glinted like gold when scraped, and was almost the same length as the other. As we lost the dinghy anchor that day, I fastened

---

20 A musket from the Spanish warship covered by the growth of coral since she sank in 1641.

21 A bronze fastening from the wreck, and what looked like just a piece of coral.

22 Inside that piece of coral was a cross of gold.

H

them together with a jubilee clip and they took its place. If they turned out to be made of gold, then we were probably the only people in the world using bullion as ground tackle.

I risked a bigger charge than usual. This time we found ourselves in a cave about five feet high and maybe fifteen long —very eerie. Nothing grew in there. The mysterious crack, however, had now trebled in size. I was sure we were now in the bowels of the vessel, and that it was only a matter of two or three charges more and we would know if there was anything there.

We were beginning to feel excited. Success was staring us in the face—but the explosives were running out. I was certain that this was the hold. It only remained to discover something in it—anything. Perhaps we already had some of its gold with the metal on the dinghy anchor. It was yellow, it glinted, it was soft, a blunt knife could peel off a sliver without effort, it was approximately eight pounds in weight, so worth over £2,000 sterling—if only it was gold.

I cursed myself for not being prepared to carry out tests.

A further blast opened up another small chamber-like space, not as large as the first. This time we combed every inch, all the way in—the top, the bottom, even to the loose gravel-like pieces at our feet.

Nothing!

We had only enough for two more charges, so I decided that we should first bring back to *Charon* all the loose bits of rock and coral lying about, and study them in the light.

The painful job began of filling sacks with sand, shells, pieces of crumbling coral, and then floating them back to the boat on air bags.

Hugh was left with it all, carefully sifting it through chicken-wire and cheese-cloth, finally washing it down with buckets of sea water. Nothing was left to chance; if even a needle lay lost in the debris, we could be sure that it would be found.

At the end of the day he had nothing to show for all the

expended labour except a curious object. Heavy and metallic, somewhat like a large peanut, one end was jagged and glinted yellow. Hugh got to work on it with an old tooth-brush, but, making little progress, he started with the wire brush—usually used for cleaning off old paint on the vessel's bottom. It began to show form, probably a fastening of some kind I thought.

"Why, it's a finger: you can see the nail!" Jill exclaimed.

"A life-size golden finger!" murmured Hugh in wonderment.

I looked carefully. Definitely it was a fine casting—a human finger without doubt. But had it been blown off by the explosion, or previously cut off by some other agency? The jagged end looked fresh, but the finger had been squashed just there a long time ago.

"I say it's gold," I hazarded. "I don't know about the bars, but this must be gold. Perhaps part of a religious figure which could still be down there, but it was damaged in the wreck by the look of the flat end. Maybe we'll find another piece of it. On the other hand, the rest would be thicker and stronger and less likely to be damaged."

Now that we were close to a possible fortune, the next few moves had to be carefully thought out. Minute examination of the sides and top where the coral had been split by the explosion revealed nothing. Somewhere lay another piece of that finger—perhaps with a whole statue on the end of it.

On one side a layer of coral gave the impression that a space could be beyond it; on the other, a crack. Which was it to be? We only had enough explosive to open up one of them, not both. The pick on its own was useless; in any case, petrol for the compressor was running low.

"Well, there we are," I explained at dinner that night. "What do we blast? Port or starboard side?"

Jill was wearing her red scarf that night. Hugh looked at it and gallantly said: "Port it is!"

And so the next few dives were concentrated on boring shot holes on the left-hand side of our cave. Later, I was often to wonder what would have happened if Jill had been wearing her green scarf, the colour for starboard. Such is the whim of fate!

Even a twin, heavy duty cylinder air-breathing set does not last long when struggling seventy-five feet down with a heavy crowbar. In, twist, out . . . In, twist, out . . . The coral was as hard as granite. Occasionally the bar hit a crumbly bit and drove in two or three inches in one go. If it is too crumbly, then it is no good for the charge, as the blast will always take the line of least resistenace.

We had only a few sticks of explosives left. This had to be the last try: all or nothing. The vault-like roof looked as if it could take it.

Jill found a hand-beaten bronze fastening amongst the rubble—another encouragement.

*   *   *

When the time came, it was one of those blue days. Jill felt ill, Hugh complained of stomach cramps, I had a hangover, which would have been fine except that all I had drunk the night before was tea with lemon juice. The *Charon* was rolling badly in some new kind of cross swell.

My first attempt at lighting the fuse failed. Somehow I dipped the match-box into the water. Back with a new box, but the fuse was wet so I had to change it. It eventually went off. We waited until after lunch for the dust to settle and for the sharks to finish off the stunned fish. These were few now; instead we had barracuda, some of which came much too close. The crack was wide enough to squeeze through. Inside came disappointment; instead of a large hold space, all there was seemed to be a narrow tunnel, and peering at the other end I could see daylight.

I switched off the torch, and light appeared in several places. We had burrowed right through the mound of coral, and another charge would have seen us out of the other side. I looked carefully around and saw a heap of coral on the other-wise flat bottom. I banged it with the chipping hammer. Some of the coral fell, revealing a mass of coins stuck on top of each other. Jill's eyes almost fell out of her head. I motioned for her to put the mass in the bag and take them outside, but they seemed stuck to the bottom. A bit more bashing with the hammer and the lot came off in one solid piece. Leaving Jill to it, I slowly examined every inch; solid coral and stone with a little sand that had filtered in somehow—that was all. I cast an envious look at the other crack, but nothing could be done about that without more explosives.

Outside the cave, Jill was waiting with the air bag. I levered off a couple of coins and broke them apart. The coral fell off them like a crust.

There was no mistaking that glint this time. They were gold.

We had made it at last. Sailed across the Atlantic in a thirty-foot boat, found our way through the maze of reefs to the wreck, and recovered a golden treasure.

Some people have been happy just to cross the Atlantic; others would no doubt settle for finding one little coin. But we had done both, and not just one little coin, but a whole heap.

For ages two years back, Jill and I had spent long nights planning what we would do if ever we found the treasure. We had purchased the yacht and sunk all the money we could get our hands on into what most people thought was a crazy adventure. We had barely enough cash left to see us back in Europe, and would have been forced to sell *Charon* to pay back various loans.

But now all that was behind us.

*　　　*　　　*

"Spanish gold," gloated Hugh, breaking up the pile and cleaning off the coral growth. "How much more is there?"

"There's bound to be more, a lot more, but not where we can get at it now. We need to remove a few more tons of coral." And then I explained that unfortunately we would have to sail to Kingston and pick up supplies, especially explosives. Our canned goods were holding out, but all fresh vegetables were

long gone. We had beans and rice unlimited, and water for
another month.

"I don't think your tomatoes will be ready in time," Jill
laughed, referring to Hugh's tomato plants blooming, by some
miracle, in a plastic bucket.

"A cup of water a day is all they're getting," Hugh used to
say, gazing at them fondly, spraying them carefully with DDT
against some non-existent bug.

I had one nagging worry. Would the Jamaican Government
let us land the treasure, or would they claim it under some
obscure treasure trove act? Before sailing from England, I had
written asking about this, and received the reply: "You will
appreciate that the enquiries which we have made of our King
Street branch are probably unique in their experience, and it
may take some little time . . ."

Then, later: "We would be obliged if you would provide us
with the following information before the treasure is trans-
shipped: The origin of the shipment; if this is not available,
evidence of the exact location of the discovery . . ." The origin
was doubtful. Was this *La Nuestra Senora de la Concepcion*? Or
was it the remains of a pirate ship, one of the hundreds operating out of Isla Tortuga in those times?

As to the exact location, those precious sightings which I
religiously took daily, and from which all possible error had
been eliminated, these were now committed to memory, there
they would stay.

Before leaving England legal points had not mattered. First
find the treasure and then we can worry about it, had been the
philosophy.

We discussed the question over the evening meal, and it
was then that we realized that in our excitement we had over-
looked something else. We were feeling very much off colour, Jill
the worst of all.

"Food poisoning, without doubt," was Hugh's verdict. I
agreed; my knees were giving way and strange cramps attacked
my legs and feet. We dosed ourselves up from the extensive

medical kit, which so far, apart from Jill's scalding, had only dealt in cuts and bruises and the occasional burns from fire-coral or other mysterious under-water pests.

I went up on deck. Hugh was already there.

"How are you feeling?" I asked.

"Bloody!" he replied.

About the way I was feeling. Heavy waves were coming over the reef, and together with the wind made a very uncomfortable and frightening motion. The night was dark; we were surrounded by jagged coral. There was no possibility of getting out. We had to ride it out until daylight.

The movement became worse. Then Hugh's voice yelled above the wind: "The starboard cable's parted!"

I had a quick look. The nylon had chafed right through; one anchor was gone, but what was worse, we were being set on to a particularly nasty coral-head—not that we could see it, but we knew of it as one of our hazards. I thought of our third anchor, but it was too light to be of any use. Only one thing left. I went below and got the anti-tank rifle. It had not done us any good so far but now it had a chance. I lashed to it one end of our spare stainless steel wire, kept in case of rigging troubles; Hugh bound a length of nylon on the other end. The gun weighed at least sixty pounds and was bound to foul up in the bottom.

"*La Nuestra . . .*" herself, I remembered uncomfortably, used her cannons for the same purpose, but foundered just the same. With the engine at full throttle I tried to manœuvre the vessel as far over towards our lost anchor as possible, while Hugh slackened off the stern line. Dashing forward, Hugh cast his beloved weapon into the deep; the wind blew us back to our old position, as Hugh let out the line.

"She won't hold . . . Yes, she's holding . . . No! Yes! She must be stuck!"

I crossed my fingers and hoped for the best.

Daylight took a long time coming. Each crunch as the chain came taut left my stomach hanging, as it were, over a chasm.

The main reef was barely discernible when the stern line finally gave way. The *Charon* swung out with the anti-tank gun taking the full weight of the vessel; there was still not enough light to try and get out to sea. Just the thought of attempting to move under these conditions made me feel weak at the knees; it was going to be touch and go at the best. If we became ship-wrecked here, there would be so little hope of getting out alive.

Jill was very ill, but she appeared and asked if there was anything she could do.

"Get the treasure into a sail-bag, the ship's papers, money, passports, etc. . . ."

She knew what that meant. I handed over control to Hugh and, going below, brought the bag up and fastened it to the Avon dinghy on the coach-house roof. The survival kit was already securely fastened on the other side.

Now I was back at the controls—a little ahead here, a bit to port . . . a bit to starboard . . . an hour went by. Hugh had already started the shackle on the main chain, in case we had to slip the lot and go. It was a risky procedure, as it would leave us with only a light anchor next time we needed to stop.

I hoped that the wind would drop and give us a chance to recover the anchor lost in the night. The anti-tank gun, I knew, would be now twisted into an interesting shape, no longer of use except in an emergency. But no, the swell increased. The engine was powerful enough if only I could see where to go. The sun came up, well hidden by the clouds. I had often visualized the route out, in fact, a well-drawn plan with bearings lay on the seat beside me, but following it was another matter.

"Start pulling her in!" I called out, easing the boat forward gently, as Hugh started to gather in the chain, waving me to the side most convenient for his labour.

"Off the bottom," Hugh announced after a nerve-shattering half-hour.

It was the point of no return. Slowly I turned *Charon* to sidle round the coral-head before entering the narrow passage, with its six-feet depth of water. There was always the nagging fear in the back of my mind that the six-feet depth might be reduced to quite a lot less by the swell. I steeled myself for that crunching feeling, ready to give the engine its all and clear over the obstruction before the next wave came.

It was just as well, for as I turned, the wind caught her; seeing that I could never make the passage, but would instead crash head on into the reef, I turned hard over, missing everything by a hair's breadth, slapped her into full astern and the full ahead. A sharp shudder passed through the *Charon* as the stern hit the reef, the throttle no longer responding in its usual way.

"Up with the jib!" I yelled, but there was no need. Hugh was already hauling it up. We shot into the passage and out the other side.

The gods must have been with us that day. Seldom have I seen more menacing reefs passing so close, while others were waiting in front. I saw Hugh once turn his back and hunch up his shoulders, waiting for the crash which never came, only by the grace of *Charon*'s designer, who made it nine feet wide and not nine feet and one inch. Coming to a clear area with a sandy bottom and a lee, we dropped our hook and went below to get the whisky bottle.

Jill was lying down, obviously with a high temperature. Hugh and I, now that the excitement was over, were both suffering. We agreed to spend the night there, and then go on to Jamaica. We all took some much-needed rest, leaving anchor watch to our guardian angel.

Jill was up and about before Hugh and I. She said that she felt better and made the coffee. Soon afterwards we weighed anchor and were off.

The wind was strong and the swell heavy, but it was not as bad as the day before. By the next dawn we were skirting the northern coast of Haiti.

Jill was down again, and seemed to be delirious; Hugh complained of stomach cramps, and my legs kept folding up on me. On top of this we had to pump every hour. Water was

coming into the skeg where it had hit the coral outcrop. The
self-steering rudder had also been sheered off in the accident.
It would only have been a matter of a few hours to fit the spare
rudder which I had made in Ponce, but I decided against it to
save time. Yet, with us all suffering from some kind of food
poisoning, self-steering had become a necessity. Hugh suggested
anchoring in the lee of the land to rest and repair the damage. I
did not know exactly where we were, but one bay looked
sheltered enough. Port Royal was only a couple of days
away.

It seemed sensible, especially in our state. We sailed round,
and a few miles further on found a smaller bay, open only to
the north and north-west. Not wanting to approach too closely
without an engine, we decided to drop the hook.

An overwhelming lethargy seemed to take hold, and it was
with an effort that I donned my wet suit and went over the
side to have a look at the skeg. The damage was not much; a
few hours' work with the fibreglass repair kit would put it
right if only the stern were out of water. Meanwhile, I stuffed
some engine-room rags into the jagged hole, then tried to take
off the propeller which was badly bent. The spare propeller
would have taken scarcely a couple of minutes to slip on, if
only I could get the damaged one off. Again there was no luck,
as the rudder was too close and the shaft seemed slightly bent
as well. We could no longer count on an engine, except perhaps
to use in an absolute emergency for a few minutes.

The self-steering rudder was my only success; the pieces just
fell away as soon as I unscrewed the three holding bolts. It
only remained to fit the new one, but I had had enough for the
day.

Hugh received the news stoically. "She won't be the first
ship without an engine, and the rags should keep out most of
the water. It doesn't sound as if that can get worse. Something
to be said for fibreglass; when you hit I thought we'd lost the
stern. But what about the lass? She seems very sick."

"Let's see how we all feel in the morning, then if she's no

better we'll signal a passing vessel in the Passage. Bound to be a few there."

It seemed the only answer, and with that we partook of some bully-beef and biscuits before going below.

*   *   *

I slept pretty soundly following a night passage, but after months at sea one develops a kind of sixth sense. Dreaming that I was adrift, I saw a large vessel bearing straight down on me. I paddled like a maniac to get out of the way, but she came on faster and faster, pushing a monstrous bow wave in front like a giant waterfall. I grew smaller and smaller until all was lost; I felt the shock as she hit, then was sent spinning into some kind of vacuum with no sound and no feeling. An eternity went by, then I came to.

I was suddenly wide awake, sitting up on the forward bunk. I felt a slight bump against the hull as if we were touching some floating object.

A strangled cry came from the stern; I felt sweat ooze out, something malevolent was on board. Leaping up, I stuck my head out of the forward hatch. Some kind of scuffling was taking place near the cockpit. The loaded compressed-air spear-gun lay with my diving gear, close by on the deck where I had left it the night before after examining the stern. I grabbed it and rushed down.

It was dark and cloudy, but not so dark that I could not see Hugh fall soundlessly into the cockpit, with a large dark shape looming over him. Of course a spear-gun should *never* be left loaded on board a yacht: in fact, it should be unloaded *before* returning on board. But this had been an exceptional case, luckily as it happened, as I had been too tired after diving the night before to go to the trouble of following the rules. Something glinted as the figure turned towards me. I pointed the spear-gun, and with the end about a foot away pressed the trigger.

A frightful shriek rent the air. I felt my hair stand on end, my sweat went cold. A spitting countenance was revealed for an instant before, with a loud gurgle, it fell backwards, and with a noisy splash disappeared over the side, tearing the gun out of my hands.

I bent over Hugh who was huddled on the cockpit seat groaning to himself. Suddenly I realized that someone else was standing up near the bows. I dashed below and picked up the shotgun—fortunately kept loaded with SG (a heavy shot suitable for deer). With the cartridge belt over my arm, I raced back just in time to see a large rowing boat push off from where it had been quietly lying under our bows. I took careful aim, and fired. A loud splash confirmed that I had scored. I fired again —loud yells came out of the darkness.

Reloading as quickly as possible, I sent another five or six shots in the general direction of the drifting boat. Then I turned back to Hugh, who I found in a bad way.

I half-carried him into the saloon and laid him on the bunk opposite Jill, who seemed unconscious. Perhaps it was just as well in the circumstances. He seemed to have trouble in breathing. Blood trickled out of the corner of his mouth, and when I looked under his blood-soaked shirt I found a small slit between two ribs, edged with rust streaks, pink froth oozing at the edges.

This was a real disaster, but a stupid thing. Probably these men were only natives who had come to steal what they could; had they not been surprised on deck, they would not doubt have been only too glad to run. Instead there was Hugh, gravely hurt and perhaps dying.

Yet in some strange way, Hugh had almost brought about his own fate. It had been his idea to anchor here rather than sail on to a safer area.

It reminded me of an old Arab story. A servant saw Death walking in the market-place, and informed his master, who feeling that his time had perhaps come, leapt on his horse and feverishly galloped to Samarra some many leagues away. That night the servant saw Death coming towards him, who said: "How surprised I am to see you here: I thought you

were with your master in Samarra, with whom I have an
appointment tonight."

"Don't move, Hugh," I told him. "I'll sail first thing in the
morning as soon as I can see. I'll stop the first ship—you'll be
O.K."

"Whisky," was all he answered.

Should I—or shouldn't I? Frankly, I just did not know if
alcohol was bad for a lung puncture; but nevertheless I gave
him a large tumbler in lieu of an anaesthetic. I then taped a
gauze pad on to the wound: there was almost no blood, and I
hoped it would work out. We had plenty of oral penicillin. I
crossed my fingers and started him off with a 250 mg. tablet
in case of infection. He swallowed it down with the whisky,
then seemed to settle down to sleep.

Back on deck the whole thing seemed like a bad dream.
We were within ten hours of a main shipping route if the wind
was right, which was almost a hundred per cent certainty with
the Trades. Yet we had no engine, no self-steering, and a leak
which required pumping at least every three hours.

Jill was sick, perhaps very sick; it was an incredible situation
for anyone else to comprehend.

It was 1967. Rockets were heading for the moon, and atomic
power commonplace; we were within shouting range of one
of the greatest nations on earth, yet we were anchored off a
republic headed by a Voodoo worshipper kept in power by a
gang of thugs, its people beaten, tortured, murdered *ad lib.*,
with law and order existing only on paper.

If I sailed to the nearest port and complained, we would
probably all be slung in jail, or worse. Next to that, not very
far away, lay the Dominican Republic, in which there had
just been a revolution. A yacht calling in there took the risk of
being taken as a gun-runner. And yet a little further on, was
Cuba—the most civilized of the three—but again not the place
for yachts. How can people living in this area of the world have
the audacity to talk of Europe as 'finished' and 'decadent'! I
thought of President Johnson's declaration: "Every day I

wake up and thank God I'm an American." It seemed to me
that he had not shopped around very much. As for the Evan-
gelical Groups beaming their daily message at great cost from
some Florida commercial station, bringing Christ to Haiti, they
would have been better employed using some of that Napalm
their countrymen were pouring out over Vietnam, to bring
back law and order to what was once a tourist paradise.

Meanwhile, we were in a bloody mess. A radio transmitter
would have been useful, but we did not carry one; even the
receiver had packed up due to a wave coming through the
open port the night of the escape from the reef. Jill's watch
had stopped; it was a self-winder and she had taken it off
when she took to her bunk. Then I noticed that my watch had
also stopped. I must have bumped it in the excitement. So we
had no time and no means of picking it up. That put paid to
any sight-taking or navigating, except by dead reckoning.

I sat until dawn, with shotgun loaded and the ammunition
ready; the Verey light pistol also at hand with half the cart-
ridges filled with bird-shot instead of flares to make a lethal
weapon at close quarters; the smaller compressed-air spear-gun
lay hidden near the bows, just in case.

Hugh started coughing badly before dawn. He had difficulty
in breathing. Jill woke up and seemed dazed and rather puzzled
that Hugh should be there.

"I took a sleeping pill, I thought that it would help," she
said.

"That explains it—I thought you were unconscious."
Quickly I explained what had happened. Her eyes opened wide
with horror. "What shall we do?"

"Leave it to me for the moment. If you are still feeling ill,
go and take it easy in the forward cabin. I'll look after Hugh
—he'll be all right." That was what I was hoping, anyway.

Jill got up, but was obviously too sick to do anything except
go back to bed. Hugh sounded terrible, and then I realized
what was wrong—the blood must have been pouring into his
lung. By taping the wound I stopped the bleeding externally

but not internally. On the other hand, if I opened the wound to drain it, he might asphyxiate for lack of air.

I gave him another 250 mg. of penicillin, and decided to drain the wound, as he seemed unable to breathe. A thin plastic tube which I had once purchased for fuel transfer, and which had turned out to be too small, seemed right for the job. I dropped it into boiling water, wondering what difference this would make as he had been stabbed with a very unclean weapon, judging by rust marks on the skin. I then took off the gauze and had a good look at the wound. It looked purplish, but almost closed; perhaps it was not so bad after all. I tried to open it a little, but Hugh objected. I gave him the whisky bottle to hang on to, then tried again. A blood-tinted liquid came out, and I intended to insert the tube; but my lack of knowledge as to whether this was the proper move halted me, so I decided to leave this unpleasant task until later.

"It's not hurting much, but I can't breathe properly," he said spluttering.

"You'll be all right," I told him, without much conviction. It seemed incredible to think that this might not be true. After all, hundreds of ships were bound to be on their way through Windward Passage.

I made coffee, peering out meanwhile, ready for more visitors. As soon as the sun came up I set my watch to an approximate time and started to pull up the anchor chain; but my luck was out. The anchor was well and truly stuck. I thought of letting it go altogether, but that would leave us ripe for some dangerous situations later on. It meant diving to clear it; the water was like soup, as a river mouth must have been close. Just the thing for sharks. I closed my mind to various possibilities, and went over the side. By touch alone, I realized that it was a job for an aqualung. They were all empty. I pulled out the compressor and saw that we had barely enough petrol in the tank. The engine started and went for about twenty minutes before packing up.

Hugh called to ask what was the matter. I told him, and he

cursed the anchor in between coughs, which I thought was a good sign.

It was one of those days. No sooner was the anchor on deck and the genoa hauled up, than I found with a shock that the pin holding the rudder to the tiller arm had fallen out, leaving the rudder stock showing a bare half-inch above the trunk. All it needed was a sudden swell in the water, out she would pop, and in would come a lot of water. Also we would be rudderless. I grabbed the piece still showing and lashed some parachute cord to it, leapt on deck, dropped the hook again, and then the genoa: back to the rudder and made a more substantial lashing, then over the side and forced the rudder back up—or rather tried to—but first had to slacken the stuffing nut.

And so it went on.

Running with sweat, I finally got *Charon* under way and we made in the direction of Isla Tortuga, the once notorious pirate haunt of the Indies. I meant to give it a wide berth, our luck was not good enough to risk meeting one of Haiti's few patrol craft.

*   *   *

The next twenty-four hours I would rather forget.

Hugh choked periodically. I tried to drain the wound without much success and without knowing if I was doing good or bad. Jill became delirious; I felt very ill, and by the next dawn did not know if I was passing out myself or was just tired out by the long night. I thought I saw a ship's lights, but when I peered with the binoculars, saw nothing at all.

Somehow I was set to the north and missed Tortuga altogether. The wind dropped, and the humidity rose. Hugh lay in a pool of sweat, and I considered moving him on deck.

---

23 Golden treasure from the wreck.

24 This solid gold finger could well have been part of a life-size religious figure, believed to have been aboard *La Nuestra Senora de la Concepcion* when she sank on Silver Reef.

At times he swore he would go himself, then he went into a kind of coma. When possible I gave him penicillin washed down with whisky.

Jill came up around dawn and said that Hugh seemed to be sleeping peacefully. She felt better, she said, and wanted to take the helm for a while. But a few minutes later she felt faint, and had to go below.

I went down to see Hugh, and again to pump the bilges. He looked very peaceful: too peaceful. Hugh was dead. It was too much to die for so little, so close to countless trained personnel who probably could have fixed him up in a few days.

I checked carefully in case he had only fainted, but there was no breath and no pulse. I wiped the blood from his mouth and straightened him up. Any minute and his eyes would open, I thought: the flapping sail brought me back to reality. I still had to find a passing vessel urgently. Hugh was past help, but Jill needed attention. Later I tried a noon position and found that we had been set to the nor'ward, no doubt by the current from the Passage.

Jill came back and said that Hugh seemed to be better.

I told her: "I'm sorry, Jill, but he's not sleeping—he's dead —and frankly I don't know what to do about it."

Jill could not believe it, but after having a closer look at Hugh, she wept and agreed that it must be so. By evening the heat was unbearable; the wind was almost nil, so we ghosted along with a genoa and nothing else. I had to make a decision. Hugh had to go. I went below, leaving Jill—who, shocked, seemed to be feeling better—and sewed him up in a sheet. Bibles did not mean much to Hugh; whisky was his one pleasure together with his beloved book of Robbie Burns—so I buried them together, as a warrior of old might have been interred with his favourite weapons.

I went forward and hacksawed off six fathoms of anchor

---

25 While repairing *Charon of Styx* on a desert island food of various sorts is found among the rocks.

chain. I did not want Jill to help me with the sad task, and asked her to get some sheets in the forward cabin. Meanwhile, I carried him to the deck and finished the job, wrapping the chain round his middle.

"I don't know the procedure, but Hugh was a friend of ours: he'd understand. All I can say is if there is a God, then let Him see to it that Hugh finds convivial company wherever he might be. The world is one good Scotsman less." And, with that, Hugh was committed to the deep he had loved so much for so long.

Seven

*"Falcon-Barker and Jill landed
on a tiny uninhabited island in the Bahamas
which they later learned was called
Little Inagua"*

SUNDAY EXPRESS August 13th, 1967

Hugh was gone, and with him the thrill of the treasure hunt lost its flavour. To go on to Jamaica and refit was unpalatable. I thought for a minute, then looked at the chart. Back to the U.K. I decided—the fun is over. To hell with it all!

The trade winds would take us through the Bahamas and along the sailing ship route. We could effect repairs at the first port of call and stock up for the return trip.

And what of the gold coins lying below the sail locker floor? I wished that we had never seen them. Hugh would never spend his share, and he had no one—not one solitary soul to leave it to, unless it was to something like the Scottish Nationalist Party.

I felt sick at heart and, giving the helm a vicious tug, altered course to the north-west. Without the right time, accurate navigation was difficult. I could manage noon sights which give latitude, but only if the sun happened to be visible just before it appeared to dip below the horizon on the sextant mirror.

It was cloudy weather and the sun only appeared intermittently, always to disappear at the crucial moment. The hurricane season was now a month old. I watched the barometer carefully for any unusual signs; the lack of wind was particularly worrying as hurricanes seldom appear when the trade winds are steady. Jill seemed much better, and so was I. For that we could be thankful.

We were somewhere near Great Inagua or Caicos, and only a miracle would see us through without running into one or the other. The only answer was to heave to at night, sailing in a westerly direction in the daytime; this left us at the mercy of unknown currents presumably setting north into the Caicos passage.

We did not mention Hugh, but his presence could still be felt. I had the uncanny feeling that during the night he was on the bows quietly smoking his pipe and keeping watch. Jill even made him a cup of coffee early one morning. Once I dozed off at the helm and woke to the sound of the genoa being hoisted; I could not remember doing it, and yet there it was—the astonishing thing being that the halyard was belayed to the cleat in Hugh's seamanlike manner, and not in my usual under and over, to-hell-with-it kind of way.

Lack of sleep and the strain of the last few days probably accounted for these peculiarities.

Hector, the idiot bird, seemed seasick and could not hold his food down; wet bread, dried fish, even powdered milk, all were jettisoned within minutes. Every now and again he would climb from the cockpit floor, using his beak like a parrot, with his tiny webbed feet flapping weakly behind him; then he would rise on his toes and flap his wings for all he was worth. Surprised to find himself still earthbound, he would flop back dejected, and doze for a while until the fit took him to have another try.

Hugh's four tomato plants, so assiduously tended and watered daily from our precious supply, had been so beautifully healthy and green-looking in the red plastic bucket, that it was with shock that we beheld them limp and half decomposed against the earth, almost as if with Hugh's passing they had also died.

Perhaps we were getting morbid, but Hugh was heavy on our minds.

Hector's predicament made me decide to try for some fresh fish so I trailed the tiny spoon; it was the last of the dozen we had purchased in Falmouth for a few pennies.

"That way, if we catch a fish, we'll know that we're close to land," I said jokingly.

It was true enough that by some strange quirk of fate we always had a catch when making a landfall. Half an hour later I was hauling in a dolphin and had no sooner gaffed it than Jill yelled: "Land, glorious land!" No more than three miles away, a low-lying strip of sand and rock was showing above the horizon. It seemed to be covered with brushwood, and having a closer look I noticed a heavy breaking sea only a mile or so ahead of our bows. Coral reefs were in profusion.

I altered course. Slowly we moved round the land until we were to leeward, then cautiously we made the approach, with anchor ready and nerves on edge; but we need not have worried. About 150 yards away from a sandy beach, in fifteen feet of crystal clear water, we anchored.

Only then did we realize just how exhausted we were.

* * *

Jill had visibly lost weight, I noted, and to my surprise she informed me that my face was white and that she could count my ribs.

Hector seemed restive. I picked him up and found that he also had suffered. Thinking that he might die during the night, I launched the dinghy and took him ashore. There, in an upturned whisky case with strips of our newly caught fish, I left him and returned on board. Jill was already fast asleep. I threw the small anchor and most of its nylon line over as an added precaution, and falling on the bunk left the hardships and sadness of the last few days behind.

It was noon the next day when the sound of birds woke me. The *Charon* felt snug and lay perfectly still, as the fresh breeze blew gently through the open hatch. I rose and peered at 'our' island. Taking the binoculars, I observed three donkeys sedately making their way round the beach. Further towards the point, bundles of pink drew my attention. A close look revealed seven pink flamingoes feeding amongst the rocks. A flight of ducks came over the trees and landed somewhere inland. White herons, overgrown water-hens, birds with long beaks, birds with short beaks—we seemed to be in a bird paradise.

"Robinson Crusoe's island," Jill said, coming out of the saloon.

"Why not? I wonder where we are. If the sun stays out I'll get a latitude."

But I was in no hurry. The main thing was that we were sheltered from prevailing winds. I was not going to shift from this wonderful spot until the propeller had been changed. How it would be done I did not know, but one thing was sure: when we sailed from Robinson Crusoe's island it would be in a sea-worthy condition. Jill was anxious to explore, and so armed with the shotgun we headed for the shore.

The reason for the bird-life was soon discovered: a small lagoon lay just over the trees. One of the three donkeys appeared and became greatly excited, peering at us through the bushes.

"It looks wild to me. I wonder if this is inhabited?" Jill wanted to know.

"If it's Little Inagua, then it isn't, and there are wild goats as well. The only other uninhabited place around here is West Caicos, and I'm sure that this isn't it," I said, showing off my knowledge.

One thing was worrying me. Officially, we should not be ashore, as we required to be 'cleared' in one of the entry ports before being allowed to wander at will. But as we were obviously in distress, we would come under some special clause. In any case, proceeding without an engine in these waters was tempting fate.

Tired and hungry we returned on board, but not before I had marked out a spot where the *Charon* could be beached. We only drew three feet eleven inches, and the tidal range was up to three feet nine, just enough to do the job, I reckoned.

The next day was spent in exploring the sea resources so as to conserve our rations.

To our amazement, in the pools amongst the reefs near the beach, ten-pound spiny lobsters abounded. So did every kind of fish, including barracuda; these we decided to leave well alone, our illnesses having hit us the day after eating one of them on the Silver Reef.

So began a daily routine: first a hunt for fish, lobster, or duck to see us through the day, then work on *Charon* until dark. As the vessel would be on the beach for some days lying at too much of a tilt for comfort, we decided to build a camp ashore.

We used sheets as a roof to keep the sun off, the plankton nets to keep out the mosquitoes which swarmed at night, and made a fireplace lined with coral. We burnt wood on top of this until the rocks became hot, then brushed away the ashes and on the gentle even heat remaining large spiny lobsters were baked in their shells to a delicious consistency in a few minutes.

Robinson Crusoe's island was becoming a reality.

Getting carried away with it all, I even planted some dried beans and tomato seeds from a few remains found under the forward bunk, besides peppers which Jill had preserved by drying. We watered them daily from the lagoon and the beans did well in the mixture of sand and donkey manure, but the rest were a failure.

Getting the *Charon* aground was fairly easy. I then used the two large inflation bags, originally designed to keep aircraft afloat in an emergency, but which had been previously so useful for removing heavy lumps of coral on the diving site. They were lashed under the stern and inflated with the compressor running on a mixture of methylated spirits, kerosene, and lub oil.

At high water *Charon* gained a few more inches. First the self-steering rudder was fitted, then work started on the propeller. It was no fun getting the twisted mass off. The wheel puller would not fit, but using compressed air and gas, I managed to make a blow-torch and used heat to get it unstuck. The new propeller was tightened up, but then I discovered that the shaft was bent. Straightening a shaft is not exactly child's play, but the blow-torch came in handy, as did large baulks of timber lying on the beach, and an old car jack.

The shaft looked as good as new, and the stern gear was fully reassembled, when a drop in barometric pressure reminded us that without a radio we had no means of obtaining hurricane warnings. I know next to nothing about electronics, but what did I have to lose? After a few days of fiddling, wiping wires, checking the connections, rather to my surprise the sound of music suddenly blared out. It was something about 'Mocking birds trilling somewhere or other': a Miami commercial station —just what we wanted. Not daring to touch anything further, we religiously kept the set on this station.

And did we regret it. Apparently, the listeners were made up of lovers of hearts and flowers, peace and goodwill to all men—that kind of thing—interrupted every half-hour by details of the latest casualties in Vietnam, and commercials.

As a light relief, a laughing hollow voice would repeat: "I am feeling very well today. My, what a fine day it is—I have never felt better," following up with a record entitled 'Graduation Day' or 'Campus Life For Ever'. But they gave weather forecasts, and included the Bahamas.

All that remained was to repair the skeg; using the fibreglass repair kit, it was an easy but dirty job.

Jill unloaded our treasure and polished the coins with Brasso. There were ninety-six coins in all, fairly worn but with the Spanish coat of arms plainly discernible; each weighed a little over half an ounce.

I tried to make out the inscription round the edges, but the letters were indistinct and the words they spelt were plainly not English. The shield with the coat of arms on one side was surmounted by a five-tipped crown; in each dip of the crown stood a cross, denoting the reign of a Catholic king; above the four crosses three three-lobed leaves, known as trefoils, surmounted the whole.

I was not well enough versed in heraldry to interpret the various symbols, but the lions rampant and various family emblems seemed to represent some kind of unity amongst the chivalry of the day, presumably the various factions of Spain were strengthening their opposition to the Arab oppressors.

The other side of the coins seemed to confirm this. A bundle of arrows lashed together were in the middle, as is still seen on practically all the military establishments of modern Spain, and this was above what looked like an Arabic design. Our coins obviously were in keeping with the historical period prior to the loss of *La Nuestra Senora de la Concepcion.* The smaller coins were devoid of any coat of arms at all, and had only an Arabic squiggle on one side with the familiar arrows on the other. A mystery seemed to be that they came from Spain and not the New World, as no gold coins were minted there before 1670. Could this mean that we had struck the skipper's private quarters? Or perhaps it had been some of the money normally carried for possible contingencies along the voyage.

The cargo should have been mainly in silver and gold ingots, loaded deep down in the holds; the area we had been working on was the stern, the traditional position for the captain's cabin, where any money for the ship would be kept.

If this were so, then the greater bulk of the vessel would be lower on the edge of the drop; in fact, it very much looked as if some of the ship's cargo must have toppled over the edge.

I could have kicked myself for not having spent more time inspecting the slope, but working deeper would have meant using more air, and our only compressor was hard put to it to charge one bottle in an hour.

Another point was that if some of the cargo had toppled over the edge, the coral would not grow at such depth, making it easier to spot any strange object.

That would be for the future to decide, and thinking about that same future, what were the laws in the Bahamas on treasure trove? For that matter, what would be the reaction of the authorities back in England?

We started to talk about it. Firstly, what of the wreck? Would we go back to it? The golden finger was life-size. Could a solid gold statue be somewhere under the coral growth, either in pieces or complete but for the fragment found? What kind of vessel was required to complete the job? A heavily built ex-fishing vessel, I thought, capable of, carrying a minimum of four large heavy anchors and plenty of chain, besides a hydraulic winch, a quarter-ton of explosives, and a pneumatic drill.

The metal detector had been a limited success, but I had ideas for improving it, and that meant constant electric power, possibly a diesel auxiliary generator. Nothing less would do than a boat fifty feet long; probably it would need to be sixty feet, and capable of at least seven knots under power.

The more we talked, the more enthusiastic we became; yet a few days before the whole venture had appeared a dismal failure. We thought of burying the treasure somewhere, taking back only a token sample until the legality of our find was certain, but later we decided to keep the lot and take the risk. So we discussed the future until darkness fell, when I slapped the final gel coat on to the skeg.

*   *   *

The *Charon* was all ready to sail, but for a few days to allow the fibreglass to cure thoroughly. If a hurricane warning came, we would take to the water immediately and head for the mangrove swamp of Acklins Island, a day or so further north; there we should be able to ride it out aground, anchors well out, and all the lines secured to whatever available points happened to be at hand.

"Now we can relax," I suggested, "and I am going to catch that white donkey and ride it. With luck, we'll be able to do a tour of the island."

Jill had been feeding the beast on some old sweet potatoes which had gone off a bit, and it now came within touching distance. It seemed to me that it could be broken in. Maybe the Robinson Crusoe stuff was getting into me as I should have known better.

We had christened the donkey 'Man Friday', and by all the rules I should have leapt on board, and later Jill and I would have had a friendly donkey to trot around our domain. As it was, when he reached for the sweet potato, I tossed a loop around his neck and threw myself on his back. For almost two seconds he acted as if this was old stuff to him; then he exploded,

Way back in my past in the State of New South Wales, I had ridden a buck-jumper called Dynamite at a local show. I earned five pounds by staying put ten seconds. A mere donkey should have been a push-over by comparison. But Man Friday was a mean bastard. First he bit me on the leg, then dashed through the mangrove, ripping me to shreds against the bracken. I thought the grand finale had come when a patch of giant cactus appeared. Apparently these must have had a bad effect on his tough hide, for he avoided them and instead flew into the lagoon.

"I've got him now," I thought. But, no! Instead of tiring himself by bucking in the mud, he let out an ear-splitting shriek and rolled over several times. When he took off after this, I was facing the wrong way holding his tail. He then took a flying leap into some coral rocks, and for a moment I thought that our positions had been reversed. Man Friday was a heavy donkey. After doing what appeared to be a *pas-de-deux* on my prostrate back, he disappeared screaming like a banshee into the bush. I never saw him again, nor wanted to.

Apart from other wounds, my ankle was swelling fast. I hobbled back to face Jill, who was highly indignant, saying that I had frightened away her donkey.

"Frightened it? My God! What about me?"

We had a set of Parke-Davis's Readi-splints, so I slipped one over the injured limb and inflated it to make a very comfortable support.

*   *   *

After two days it seemed evident that no bones were broken, but it was no use going to sea in that state. We drew *Charon* back into the deep water, and tested the engine. All was well.

I decided to have a spring-cleaning and get rid of the clutter that somehow had accumulated over the last few months.

Jill's collection of sea-shells drew my attention. "Is this really necessary?" I asked, pointing to a clam the size of a cathedral font. Apparently it was! Then a few odd-shaped coral rocks got the treatment. One in particular caught my eye; it was in the rough shape of a cross. Suddenly I had an idea, and getting the chipping hammer started to tap away at the edges. It shattered and in my hand I held a tiny, solid gold cross. We stood looking at it speechlessly, as the same thing crossed both our minds. How many other innocent-looking pieces of coral might have been hiding untold items of interest? The rest of Jill's coral collection, I regret, proved less profitable.

The cross was rough cast; either someone had amateurishly decided to make himself a crucifix and had plenty of gold on hand to do it with, or maybe he had stolen the gold and hoped to get away with it by this devious method. Perhaps a light-fingered sailor had used his spare time during the voyage manufacturing crosses for future resale.

Either way, we were richer by this new piece.

I took sights, and proved what I had hoped; we were anchored off Little Inagua Island. We decided that if the treasure came to anything worth while, we would find out if this island was for sale, as many uninhabited islands in the Bahamas seem to be.

We had seen every kind of fish except shark, and were beginning to wonder if they were scarce in these waters. That was until I went into a pool at low water, when it was no more than three feet deep, and joined to the sea by a channel of about eight or ten inches over the reef; and I saw a tail sticking out from under a rock. I fitted a flash bulb to my 'Rolleimarine' camera and crept up. The shark lay without movement, his dorsal fin over on one side, a dozen or so fish swimming unconcerned about him. It would have been ridiculous to take a shot like that, as anyone seeing the photograph would have thought the fish dead.

Then slowly he rose and took a good look at me. Sluggishly he moved round the coral, made a sudden dart at a large lobster, missed it, and in bad humour headed straight for me. He was about eight feet long, and a member of the nurse family, which are said to be harmless by many; but not by the twelve or so persons reported to have been attacked in the last few years by specimens of this fish, ranging from as little as eighteen inches to nine feet long.

I was intent on photographing him, and only when he was about a foot away did it dawn on me that this slow-moving object was actually about to try his teeth on me. His head was almost underneath my body when I brought down the camera with all my strength. It was like hitting a rock. It made him move on, however, and almost into Jill, who was hovering behind. He made a circle of the pool and then came at me again, but this time very much faster. By now I had the harpoon gun in my hand, but no time to load it. He came low down, perhaps going for my legs. I moved them upwards and jabbed hard with the gun, pretty well midway between the nasty button eyes. His tail caught my shoulder and ripped the neoprene material. He twisted and faced me. It looked as if I was in for another charge, but, changing his mind, the shark threw himself up into the half-dry channel and with a great threshing of tail made his way out over the reef.

Jill was amazed. "In this tiny pool—who would have thought it? Why, little kids could be left here without anyone thinking twice about it!"

"Looks as if somebody should invent a camera-case with a built-in spear gun, a real James Bond job," was my only comment. Sharks had ceased to surprise me. As far as I was concerned, they were all potentially dangerous.

The islands also contained, as we soon discovered, turtles whose tender flesh tasted like the finest veal; there were thousands of edible shell-fish on the shore, and in a few feet of water were conch-shells by the hundred, suitable for chowder or any kind of stew favoured by the gatherer.

"At least we shall be richer than when we left," I said to Jill as I strained over the anchor chain while she turned the helm into the wind. Hector, the bird, suddenly appeared out of the setting sun, it was the first time he had approached us since I had left him on shore. He would fly high over the *Charon* in the early mornings, giving his peculiar high-pitched calls, then disappear for the day. Now he seemed highly excited; we were his last link with the Silver Reef, and some instinct must have been bothering him. He fluttered down and hovered over the hand-rail, then circled, calling desperately. As the land receded, he made a final pass and, climbing rapidly in a sweeping turn, left for his new home.

Eight

"Death yacht vanishes in the Atlantic"

DAILY EXPRESS August, 1967

It was easy sailing once more. The trade winds blew more gently and the swell had dropped to reasonable proportions. The self-steering was doing its job magnificently.

The stern cabin where Hugh had lived his last few weeks was in a mess. It had been used as a store-room from the beginning with only enough space left for Hugh on one bunk; but since the events of the last few days everything had been thrown into confusion. I decided to clear it up before our arrival in Ragged Island—the nearest official clearance port in the Bahamas. Compressor, aqualungs, various other diving gear, paints and brushes, pieces of fibreglass and assorted cans of food, tools . . . out they all came until the cockpit was stacked high with material. I even took off the plastic-covered mattresses and laid them on the deck to air.

Purely as routine, I checked under each bunk for water. Originally some parts had been kept there, but after discovering them soaked and ruined by sea water, the space had been discontinued as a store area.

I was surprised, therefore, when I found a plastic bag full of assorted gear. It was unfamiliar, and I suddenly realized that it must have belonged to Hugh. We had buried him with his last clean shirt, his packet of private papers and his copy of Burns. It had never occurred to me that he owned much else, but there in front of my eyes were his most private possessions.

There was a broken pipe of unknown antiquity, and an old handbook on the South Americas, then a few one-pound notes,

Portuguese and Spanish money, a worn-out pair of 'flip-flops', a handkerchief, an International vaccination certificate, and the upper torn half of a French *Permit de Circulation*, usually issued as a kind of driving licence to operators of yachts in French waters.

It is a strange thing about the sea. A man can be on a ship for months; he can work, talk, eat, play cards, and sleep with a crowd, but somehow he remains alone; his inner thoughts continue pure and unperturbed. His mind governs a personal walled garden in which no one dare walk. It is totally unlike any life ashore, where in circumstances such as military service, the men get to know each other's innermost secrets; they understand one another better than their own wives or mothers will ever hope to do. Perhaps that is why reunions go on year after year, until the last grey-beard is laid to rest and the cemetery cleared for a new batch.

I had never heard this fact of the sea mentioned before, except in an allusion in another form by Joseph Conrad; but it came to me strongly at this moment that I had never really known Hugh.

I had accepted him as one accepts the wind and the sky, with no more curiosity than I normally had for my other friends.

We come and we go—who cares from what bed? What is past is finished, the sun will rise again sooner or later: why remember the cold night?

I picked up the parcel and gave it to the sea.

"What are you throwing over now?" called Jill, watching it disappear behind us.

"Just something belonging to Hugh—private papers or something," was all I replied.

It is possible that we had been away too long; we had been out of touch with civilization, and dependent only on ourselves for survival. Perhaps that was why Jill's idea seemed logical at that moment; she felt that the best thing was to forget Hugh, and carry on just as if he had never been.

It would have been Hugh's wish, I was certain, as it would have been mine in like circumstances.

Not for us the fussing minor officials, the signing of declarations, and solemn empty faces, lining up like good little marionettes waiting for the strings to be pulled.

Maybe some would enquire—"I wonder what happened to Hugh?" We could then always mention casually leaving him in the Bahamas, in the U.S.A.—in fact, anywhere. I only remember being asked twice in the whole time I had known Hugh, "How is Hugh these days?"—and that was after the newspaper publicity, and by a mutual friend who, come to think of it, was a reformed smuggler—not one to follow up any embarrassing enquiry.

The self-steering was doing its job magnificently, and so a few days later, without incident, we arrived and cleared at the tiny rock known as Ragged Island. This small community is primitive, subsisting mainly on fish with rice and beans, with a few other oddments purchased through the sale of sea salt. There are no vegetables or fruit, except for a few coconuts. As one man said with a shrug, "If we grow anything, the kids steal it, so why bother."

Everyone was friendly, yet we found that although the Commissioner responsible for the administration of the island sat under a portrait of the Queen, and the Customs man wore a cap with a large brass badge 'E.R.', her portrait on a sterling pound note with 'Bank of England' written in large flowery letters, did not cut much ice.

We felt slightly annoyed that the meagre supplies available in the local shops were denied us; so we decided that even if we had wanted to report Hugh's death, it could not have been taken seriously in such a place. However, after more thinking, we also came to the realization that Hugh's murder could not be ignored; so I made up my report in diary form for the Sunday newspaper which had contracted me before leaving the U.K.

The mail boat was fortunately, or unfortunately as it happened, calling on its usual twice-monthly visit. We posted

K

our letters and sailed out of the port, making for Georgetown.

Awaiting us there were excited cables. We had accepted Hugh's demise; it now seemed all a long time ago, but the newspaper story had created some excitement, particularly in Nassau, where a local paper used the syndicated version. Up to then, no official report had been made, so this appeared the judicious moment to do it. Unfortunately, Georgetown did not seem to be the place to explain such an adventure as ours.

I sat down and wrote a short resume of the affair to the Governor of the Bahamas, informing him that we were on our way. However, before we could sail, two police officers flew in from the capital and boarded us to get a statement; the Press descended in droves, thirsty and somewhat irked by the fact that we were anchored off and not talking.

The tone of the affair got on our nerves, and seeing the police officers drinking with the pressmen one evening, we came to the conclusion that we should go to Nassau and deal with head office. We had made our report, and nothing stood in our way until the senior police officer professed great interest in the treasure on board, 'just to look at it'.

I was wary. Who wouldn't be? "It's all been sent away," I told him. We would have much preferred the customary 'royal fifth' of old (the King usually received this as his share); but this was 1967, a Socialist Government in Britain, and taxation up to 19s. 6d. in the pound.

The police officer asked how it had been disposed of, and when. I replied: "This has nothing to do with the matter in hand, and is my business only." Whereupon he threatened to search the vessel.

I informed him that he could go ahead, but that I considered myself legally entitled to defend the vessel physically, and would use all the means at my disposal to counter an attempt to remove any object from the craft. He went ashore rather dissatisfied, and later asked that I should take an escort to Nassau with me, threatening arrest if I did not.

It may at this stage be suitable to bring in a few words on the legal aspects as to the recovery of objects of monetary value in the sea.

I would like to make it known, before starting, that these conclusions are mine entirely. As the Cantonese were sometimes fond of saying (that was before Communism came in): "He who keeps mouth shut will not drop teeth on pavement". Most countries have treasure trove laws. These are simple. All belongs to the State, which may reward you or punish you, depending on who your friends are. Treasure in the sea, however, cannot rightly be called treasure trove as it is not hidden in a private place. Whereupon, to make it all legal, each country claims that anything found in its territorial waters belongs to the State. Stymied again: the only thing left for a private individual is to make a deal with a government first. Certain areas, such as where we were operating, are considered 'international'—in other words, you become fair game to whosoever gets you first. If you get away with it, no one can call you a thief; if you do not, you can take your place at the end of the queue, and the massacred Incas would probably qualify as first in line.

Were I—as I hope to do in the future—to come upon several tons of bullion, I personally would sail non-stop to Britain and deposit it with the Bank of England, demanding protection as a British-registered vessel if necessary. In these conditions, after paying tax of some kind (one can consider this as one would an insurance premium) I would be rich and, perforce, respectable.

The Spanish Government would no doubt put in a claim on its 400-year-old property, but would get the same reply as it got on the subject of Gibraltar.

The Haitians would be ignored; no white man is safe there anyway, and any other nation would merely be asking for the traditional two-finger sign. Or, to quote another expert: "The authorities all along the Caribbean Sea are unwilling or unable to go in search of treasure, or to pay others to do so, but they lay claim immediately anyone finds the slightest thing, if they can put their hands on it." *The Gulf Stream Story*, Hans Leip, 1957.

*   *   *

Staying any longer in Georgetown, however pleasant the scenery and the hospitality of an American couple who befriended us, became pointless.

My temperament is inclined to become violent in the face of witless provocation, and, as Jill said: "It wouldn't do. Better to get out before tempers become strained further."

In the hours when most people sleep, we weighed anchor and moved out of the harbour.

Georgetown is difficult to enter in daylight, and few would attempt it in the dark. So the Press and the constabulary slept waiting for another absorbing day. By daylight we were well away, following the chain of islands to Nassau; later in the afternoon were making carefully along a rocky passage, moving into the inside route through the Galliot Cut. It was all very tricky stuff, and when a police plane repeatedly buzzed us, I I suddenly became enraged.

"So the bastards want to show that they can get us any time they want! Right, to hell with Nassau!"

Less boisterously, the thought entered my mind that once in Nassau, we would no doubt be held up and perhaps lose our hard-acquired discoveries. Once in official hands, a team of lawyers would prize it loose, and when they did, what would be left of it?

Waiting until dark I altered course, not in the direction they might imagine, but into the shallow reef-infested area leading into a deep lake-like body of water known as the Tongue of Ocean. I stayed at the bows, keeping lookout, while Jill steered, the engine ticking over in case of a sudden manœuvre. The waters varied from forty feet to six feet deep, and occasionally we passed over rocky outcrops. The sand shone in the moonlight, but when the clouds passed over it was left purely to the gods. We missed three distinct possibilities of shipwreck, and the excitement kept us on our toes; when daylight came we were completely played out.

However, we made it. We listened for aircraft during the day, and by night knew that we had given them something to think about.

We still had a long way to go, and a certain amount of adventure lay ahead. The island of Andros remained in our path and it is over a hundred miles long. If we skirted the coast heading north, we would have to pass Nassau. If we tried south, we would get stuck in the reefs and shallows of the Great Bahama Bank. Andros is split in the middle by a huge swamp, cut into many channels.

Passages can be found which eventually connect up with the sea on the other side. We had no chart, and knew from previous conversation that two feet was the average depth, while we drew four.

We entered the reef into the main channel, and went aground before dark. A week later we came out the other side.

It had been mighty interesting: weird fish and birds, no habitation, or signs of life. The only real hardship came from the stinging flies, mosquitoes, and other insects which descended in clouds. We had to wear our clothes in the clinging humid heat to protect ourselves, and at night closed the boat completely up. It was stifling. An eerie brooding area of mangrove and water, with mysterious splashes, probably from the alligators and snakes that infest the place.

The number of times we had to use the anchor to pull ourselves off were innumerable.

* * *

Forty-eight hours later we entered Port Everglades, U.S.A. We were especially pleased to read a garbled newspaper article in a Bahamian newspaper, "The yacht last sighted in the Exuma Cays, disappeared, and after almost a week of aerial searching the Royal Bahamian Police called off the hunt."

It had been a sad but great adventure, which now lay behind us like a far-away dream.

Marketing our treasure was not as easy as one would suppose. The ninety-six gold coins themselves represented about $3,000 in gold value, based on the American fixed price of $35 per ounce. The real money was to be had by finding a rich collector. Our pieces were late fifteenth century, minted in provincial Spain during the reign of Ferdinand and Elizabeth (1497–1516).

These, it seemed, were not particularly rare, and the value to a collector is much influenced by the quality of the coin; the closer to mint condition, the more the piece is worth.

Our coins were unfortunately a long way from mint condition and looked as if they had been bounced on many a tavern bench.

We also soon discovered that around every rich collector are a multitude of agents, dealers, and a few straight-out crooks who make no pretence whatever about keeping to the accepted code of law and order; when there is money to be made, even mother's gold fillings are not safe.

My first contact took it for granted that I had lifted the coins from some collector or museum in another state. He offered $4,000 for the lot, and with regret informed me that they were no doubt worth more, but the only way to be sure of this would be to go to an expert who would want to know how they were acquired.

When I explained my willingness to go to such an expert, he stated that I might be fool enough to risk going to jail, but not him.

Eventually I convinced him that they were honestly procured. It must have been his first experience with such a case, and left him somewhat at a loss.

He then asked that I call again a day later.

When I did, a blustery individual was in the office. The latter's first remark was, "Where did you get that watch? I've always wanted a watch like that—how much will you sell it to me for?"

"No, my Rolex is not for sale!"

"Are you sure?"

"Yes, I am sure!"

"Gee! I've always wanted a watch like that!"

He kept muttering, and then offered me $6,000 for the coins, I found it most intriguing that a man willing to part with $6,000 for some gold coins would not think of stepping over to a jewellery store and buy himself a mere $150 watch. But that is one of these unfathomable American quirks.

"12,000 dollars, or nothing," I replied.

One would have thought that I had kicked him in the whatsits. He felt where his heart ought to have been, gasped, popped a few pills into his mouth and washed them down with some neat Bourbon handily placed in a drawer of the desk

Meanwhile, his mate scrambled out and came back with a glass of water which was contemptuously whipped aside and trickled away into the files.

After about three hours the Bourbon was finished, and so were the pills. $7,000 was their limit. I was not prepared to settle for so little, and walked out into the sunlight with cries of "You shouldn't! Really you shouldn't!" coming from the weaker of the two, while the other's parting words were "Sure you don't want to sell that watch?"

Jill was amused, and thought that maybe I would do a really good deal if I would only throw in the watch with the coins.

It was an irritating fact that if I were prepared to advertise, and willing to travel all over the U.S.A., I would eventually get three or four times what I had been offered.

A stranger with no contacts is fair game in the mad scramble for the Almighty Dollar. One had to admit that the participants in this Twentieth Century Marathon were characters indeed; they were not the bloodless wet-handed and granite-hearted worshippers of the Almighty accountant sitting in the heavens, which one usually meets in the financial circles of Europe. No! these were men of blood and guts just as prepared to give a hand-out to the needy as a bullet to a competitor. Product of a violent society, but human still.

After an interesting two weeks, I finally settled for $10,500 for most of the loot, keeping back the gold finger and a half-dozen coins.

We met an airline pilot, who fell in love with *Charon*, which had served us so well. We let him have it for a price, glad that our vessel was in good hands, and in turn purchased a Volkswagon camper and drove off to Mexico and around the vastness of the U.S.A.

We found what a rancher told us was the last frontier. Tomato and citrus grew there in profusion. The Everglades with its mysterious waterways and unknown nocturnal creatures made a natural boundary.

We loved it and, with the proceeds of the treasure, purchased a few acres.

It had taken a long time, but we had found our home.

Epilogue

The expedition is over. You read the story. Switch out the light and go to sleep, or twist and turn wondering about those elusive loose ends. Some of them bother me too. Things are never what they seem.

It would be easy to put down the whole history of bad luck that surrounds the various attempts to salvage the gold and silver from the wreck of *La Nuestra Senora de la Concepcion* under the heading of superstition; but the truth is that it is a dangerous area and countless vessels have left their bones on the reefs.

To cruise anywhere near is bad enough, but to move in and potter around the shallows is almost suicidal. Treacherous currents, boilers where the water foams and seethes with the movement of the Atlantic swell, sudden squalls with swift rising seas which can hit any time of day or night—these are everyday occurrences. Only careful seamanship, with a good crew and a first-class deep-water vessel, could successfully undertake what we had tried to do with a small yacht and three people.

Korganoff, with all his organization and years of preparation, culminating in the obtaining of two vessels and twenty-eight persons, was still putting things together a year after the proposed sailing date. I felt sorry for him—or did I really? It's always easier to feel sorry for your opponent when you are the winner. One could be sure of one thing, Korganoff was not going to give up. He would go on, even if it took him the rest of his life. After all, life is all illusion and as long as the treasure appeared to be still lying on Silver Reef, he would be happy; he would learn of my finds with trepidation, but another sixty tons remained; that is, until my next visit.

The gangster and his mob, on the other hand, had the simplest idea of all; rather old-fashioned, of course, but well in keeping with the tradition of the Caribbean. It had been to wait for someone to recover the treasure, then take it away from them. But even they, sooner or later, would have fallen foul of a Haitian gun-boat or a Dominican coastal patrol looking for arms smugglers; perhaps even a Cuban anti-revolutionary group out to sink anything in sight. There are any number of hazards in that trigger-happy area.

As I write this story I feel an odd weariness. Most of my readers, I know, lead normal lives. They wear galoshes when it rains, sniff their inhalers when the day is cold, and possess mothers, wives and patter of little feet. The newspaper on the way to work: 'Nuns Raped in the Congo', 'Napalm Horror in Vietnam', 'Carrots cheaper this Year'; all this, when you are on a tiny boat way out at sea, just does not register. It is alien.

The nine-to-five mentality cannot even begin to comprehend that there is no telephone, no friendly police-sergeant benignly smiling at you over his desk with "Can I help you, sir?" As one reporter said to me, in a rather disapproving manner, "Some people take their murders lightly!"

Just how do you take *your* murders? Scream and call for a cup of tea? I can tell you one thing: if it's a hot day and you are on your own, you'll drag the body outside and reach for the flit-gun.

At the time of the attack on Hugh and his subsequent death, the dictator of Haiti, François ('Papa Doc') Duvalier, had just personally supervised the execution of nineteen of his officers for taking part in a plot to overthrow his rule. That he may have been on the right track is evident from the fact that, later, six persons were convicted in a U.S.A. courtroom for conspiring to invade Haiti.

A Haitian refugee, now safe in Florida, told me of armed

attacks over the Dominican border by groups of rebels. When I asked him what he thought of anchoring a small yacht near the shore, he said: "Monsieur, you would take a great risk, some people would try to steal the yacht to escape Haiti, and if they didn't the 'Tonton Macouts' [Creole for 'Bogeymen', as the security thugs are labelled] would shoot everybody on it."

Captain Lee Hall, U.S. Coastguard, licensed yacht delivery skipper of Port Everglades, Florida, once seized by the Haitian authorities on a delivery job and repatriated after considerable hardship, told me of seeing an American yacht showing machine-gun bullet holes down one side of the wheelhouse after an encounter with armed natives near the coast. They had come in close to anchor for the purpose of changing the lubricating oil in the engines.

In Washington, by chance, I met a Haitian diplomat, and cautiously tried to bring the subject around to possibilities of attacks having been made on foreign yachts in his country. First, I had to listen to a highly-coloured eulogy on the merits of 'Papa Doc', culminating with ". . . and our President is a great philosopher."

Now I know that Plato was supposed to have remarked that people could only be happy if ruled by a philosopher, and this was borne out by Marcus Aurelius; but the premiss is hardly accurate when applied to a maniac like Duvalier.

"He certainly proved Plato to be wrong," I put in.

"That's it! Greater than Plato!" He breathed ecstatically, after all of which we got on splendidly for a while.

He allowed that some desperate criminal element trying to escape just retribution might attack any small yacht imprudent enough to anchor too close to shore in a deserted area, but never ever in Port au Prince (the major port in the Haitian republic).

Now that was a laugh. As it happened, I had met a single-handed yachtsman who had called into this port. The police had taken him off his boat and after a few hours of interrogation let him go. By this time this vessel was bare of sails, ropes, instruments, and supplies. In fact, everything movable had disappeared. The police, if anything, appeared amused at his discomfiture. My diplomat did not approve of this tale and, after growling that everybody lied about Haiti, left in a huff.

Charon had done its job, but was too small for any future attempts on the treasure wreck. What was needed was a heavy sea-going work boat able to carry several tons of explosives and fitted with heavy lift gear to remove the larger lumps of coral.

We had achieved our main aim, which had been to pin-point the spot and check if anything of value was contained therein.

I started looking for a suitable vessel, but our story had got around; people bought me drinks, made dubious offers, and asked about the Silver Reef. Two diving boats in the Florida area started to fit up for an expedition, and I heard of another from Jamaica. It looked as if the north of Haiti was going to be a busy place when the hurricane season terminated in October.

For us there was no hurry. Their hope of finding our treasure in the forty square miles of reefs was less than good; so that left us as the only two people knowing where we could possibly recover a treasure large enough to outfit a palace with solid gold or silver furniture—given the right vessel and proper gear.

Soon, perhaps, we shall go back: but that will be another story. After the tribulations of our last voyage, we shall go in secrecy.

Meanwhile, we shall direct our energies into clearing that sun-baked plot of land in Florida, which our first bite at the treasure kindly afforded us, and to growing the largest oranges you have ever seen.

Index